WITHDRAWN

60
Minutes
Classics

Con Men

Fascinating Profiles
of Swindlers and
Rogues from the
Files of the
Most Successful
Broadcast in
Television History

Edited by
Ian Jackman

SIMON & SCHUSTER
:: New York :: London :: Toronto :: Sydney :: Singapore ::

SIMON & SCHUSTER
Rockefeller Center
1230 Avenue of the Americas
New York, NY 10020

Copyright © 2003 by CBS Worldwide, Inc.
All rights reserved, including the
right of reproduction in whole or
in part in any form.

SIMON & SCHUSTER and colophon
are registered trademarks of
Simon & Schuster, Inc.

For information about special discounts for bulk purchases,
please contact Simon & Schuster Special Sales at
1-800-456-6798 or business@simonandschuster.com

Designed by Sam Potts

Manufactured in the United States of America

10 9 8 7 6 5 4 3 2 1

Library of Congress Cataloging-in-Publication Data
Con men : fascinating profiles of swindlers and rogues from the files of the
most successful broadcast in television history / edited by Ian Jackman.
p.   cm
1. Swindlers and swindling—United States—Interviews. 2. Criminals—United
States—Interviews. 3. 60 minutes (Television program) 4. Interviewing on
television. I. Title: Fascinating profiles of swindlers and rogues from the files
of the most successful broadcast in television history. II. Title: At head of title:
60 minutes classics. III. Title: Sixty minutes classics. IV. Jackman, Ian.
V. 60 minutes (Television program)
HV6695 .C77   2003
364.16'3'0922—dc21   2002191141
ISBN 0-7432-2448-5

All photographs courtesy of CBS Worldwide, Inc.

Acknowledgments

Thanks to Rick Altabef, Lynn Anderson, Edith Baltazar, Bridie Clark, Barbara Dury, Nicole Graev, Don Hewitt, Josh Howard, Geoff Kloske, Alison Pepper, Emily Remes, David Rosenthal, Jonathan Sternberg, Kevin Tedesco, Mike Wallace, Jennifer Weidman, Rob Weisbach, Betsy West, and Tracy Woelfel.

For Don Hewitt and his gang

of *60 Minutes* reporters—

still the very best at exposing

the very worst

Contents

Introduction

Mike Wallace

Morley Safer said it about twenty-five years ago: A crook doesn't feel he's really made it as a crook until we've told his story on *60 Minutes.* And the plain fact is that *60 Minutes* itself hadn't really made it with America's television audience until we started telling stories about crooks, con men, and scoundrels, in the early 1970s.

When Harry Reasoner and I began the series back in 1968, we covered national and international controversies, civil rights battles, the Vietnam War. But these weren't just two- or three-minute takeouts of the *CBS Evening News.* Instead, they were fifteen-minute stories, "stories" as defined by our executive producer Don Hewitt, that focused on the characters involved, their motives, their methods of operation, their successes, and their failures.

60 Minutes itself was a *succès d'estime* in those early years, but we failed to attract the size of audience we were after—the millions who regularly watched sitcoms and dramas, westerns and variety shows, but rarely bothered with news documentaries. And when Harry departed the CBS premises in 1970 in favor of anchoring the *ABC Evening News,* we feared that a big chunk of our *60 Minutes* audience might depart with him, for he was middle America; he was the heart of America.

So Hewitt and I cast about for something fresh, something harder-edged. And we discovered (eureka!) something that there was too little of in television back then: investigative reporting. By this time, Watergate having surfaced, we joined the hunt for miscreants and flushed out a few ourselves, such as Chuck Colson, Donald Segretti, and G. Gordon Liddy. We were able to give them more time and focus than the network evening news shows could. The audience began to respond; its numbers grew. We figured that Americans might want to see not just reports of political skullduggery but tales of criminal greed, scams, and schemes. This led us to some of the most devious, entertaining, piratical, and resourceful individuals ever to grace a television screen.

One strange thing about many of these characters is that despite their inventive villainies, there's nothing about them in the flesh that would lead you to believe they would be any more conniving than the clerk who hands you pills at your local pharmacy.

The best of them, however, are the entertainers, the con men, the slicksters and storytellers who take perverse professional pride in bilking the unwary. Although it must be said that their unwary "marks," their victims, are themselves so greedy that too often they throw caution to the wind, somehow reluctant to doubt the validity of the lures dangled before them.

The titles of some of the pieces detailing the adventures of our malefactors is a descriptive catalog of what they were up to: "Mail-Order Ministers," "The Gentle Art of Forgery," "1-800-CON MAN." And the one I like best, "Wheeler, Dealer, Squealer." As you'll shortly see, we've had such a good time doing these stories—exposing their frauds, helping send some of them away to prison—that over the years, we were bound to learn the tricks of their trade. Sometimes, infrequently, it took a con to catch a con.

So in the course of investigating these stories, occasionally we turned devious ourselves, which triggered some soul-searching among us about the tactics we used to nail the bad guys. For example, is it proper to pose as someone other than a reporter to catch a crook? Is it fair for us to set up our own enterprise—a bar, a clinic, a sting operation—to lure unsuspecting subjects before our cameras, or is that entrapment?

Twenty years ago we did a full *60 Minutes* piece to try to get answers to these questions from several esteemed print journalists, from whom we caught a fair amount of flak. For example, we showed them a piece we had broadcast about how easy it could be to procure false ID documents in order to obtain a U.S. passport under a phony name. The piece had been suggested to us by Frances Knight, then head of the Passport Office in Washington, who was alarmed by the increasing nationwide use of the false ID.

Following her lead, we deployed a con woman to help us. Lucy Spiegel was a *60 Minutes* researcher at the time; it turned out that she was also a consummate actress. We followed her, our cameras rolling, into various local and state offices. Under a name not her own she managed to get herself a certified copy of a phony birth certificate, a Social Security card, a Maryland driver's license, a state unemployment card, and finally the prize we were after, a gold-embossed U.S. passport. Of course, we later returned all the illegal stuff we'd collected so that Lucy wouldn't go to jail.

A couple of the print journalists we'd asked to comment were horrified at what we'd done. Ellen Goodman of *The Boston Globe:* "You're saying that in pursuit of deceit, deceit is okay, that journalists have the right to use untruths because we are going for the greater truth."

And Gene Patterson, a crusty veteran shoe leather reporter/ editor for *The Atlanta Journal, The Washington Post,* and the *St. Petersburg Times,* was scandalized. "You're breaking the law," he told us. "The Passport Office got *60 Minutes* to do its work for it. It seems to me the story here is, why doesn't the Passport Office enforce the law?"

But Bob Greene of *Newsday,* the Long Island newspaper he has long served as investigative reporter and editor, applauded us. "It was good reporting, plain and simple," he said. "The fact that it was on camera was embarrassing to the Passport Office and showed that serious steps had to be taken to bring the illegal practice to a halt." Our audience responded similarly. Good for you, they said in effect. Get the crooks, get the con women any way you can. And in the wake of 9/11, I'm certain today's audience would be even more approving.

The first scam you'll read about, involving a certain phony medical doctor named R. J. Rudd, was a complicated venture, aimed primarily at mulcting rich old ladies. These women had ailments, real or imagined, plus a willingness to listen to Dr.

Rudd's health ministrations as well as his invitation to get in on some of his "lucrative" real estate deals. In order to get Rudd to give us, on camera, the lowdown on his scheme, we had to con him ourselves, as you will shortly learn. His tale made for fascinating television and put him out of business and into prison for a sentence of seven years.

What motivates con men (and I'm sure it's true of con women as well) to do what they do—to break the law, to take advantage of their victims? Money, of course, that's obvious. But as I think back over the years, I've come to believe that they see themselves as adventurers, smarter than lots of legitimate business types. They're thrill seekers, some of them willing to bet their savvy against considerable odds, knowing that the chances are they'll wind up in the slammer—and many of them do. But then, once inside, most of them make model prisoners, obeying the rules, giving corrections officers little trouble, so that their sentences will be shortened "for good behavior" and they'll be set free to ply their trade once again.

And *60 Minutes* will be there, too, ready to expose them.

Con Men

This Year at Murrieta

:: January 1, 1978 ::

No one is more vulnerable to a con than a person afflicted with an incurable or terminal disease. Snake oil salesmen have been around forever, preying on the desperate hopes of the sick and the infirm. On New Year's Day 1978, Mike Wallace reported on a particularly grievous representative of the species, an individual named R. J. Rudd who was running a cancer clinic at a spa in Murrieta Hot Springs, California.

After receiving a number of letters about Murrieta and conferring with California medical authorities and the local sheriff, who had looked over the place himself, *60 Minutes* decided there was enough material to support an investigation. R. J. Rudd was treated to a classic journalistic sting operation, itself a con of sorts.

The scam began when a wealthy, semiretired investment counselor who called himself "The Colonel" enrolled in the Murrieta cure program. He said he wanted treatment because he'd just learned he had leukemia. The Colonel arrived with an entourage: his concerned nephew, who was a traveling photographer by trade, and his longtime secretary.

In fact, "The Colonel" was *60 Minutes* soundman James Camery. His "nephew" was cameraman Greg Cook, and producer Marion Goldin played the role of his "secretary." The three began looking into what was going on at Murrieta, secretly filming and recording as they went. To add to the aura of affluence they wanted to establish, the threesome arrived in the international symbol of wealth, a Rolls-Royce.

R. J. Rudd

Camery paid $560 up front for a week's stay at the spa and was told he should plan on being there a minimum of two weeks. The Colonel was then seen by the Murrieta doctor, Horace Gibson. It was the only time Camery met with Dr. Gibson. In the diagnostic part of the examination, Gibson looked into Camery's eyes and told him he didn't in fact have leukemia. But Gibson did not send Camery home. Gibson diagnosed what he described as a "leaky lung" as the source of his difficulties.

Over the next few days, Camery the patient was not supervised closely. What attention he got came from the spa's "counselors" or "testers," who administered Murrieta's singular treatment. Like everyone at the spa, Camery was placed on a three-day fast during which he was given only distilled water and lemon juice. After the fast, he moved to a light vegetable diet augmented with vitamins and mineral supplements. Camery's progress was monitored by a series of saliva and urine tests administered by the counselors. None of the counselors was a medical doctor. Some were chiropractors. One said he used to sell flooring; another had been an embalmer's assistant.

Camery's urine was collected twice a day, taken away, and tested. The tests produced complicated sets of numbers. Patients were told that these numbers were fed into a computer. The results supposedly showed how patients were doing, presumably documenting their improving health.

But while Camery was apparently subsisting on the prescribed regimen of distilled water and lemon juice, he was actually eating quite well. More substantial breakfasts and lunches were brought to his room by his colleagues. There was so little supervision that the Colonel's nephew and secretary had no difficulty in taking their charge out to dinner each night. Camery was filmed enjoying a decidedly unhealthy-looking meal, complete with a glass of red wine.

The fact that Camery was not fasting should have compromised the results produced by the computer analysis of his urine. To fur-

ther test the validity of the process—or to undermine it—cameraman Greg Cook's urine was substituted for Camery's on two occasions, and once Marion Goldin provided the sample. Despite these
deceptions, Camery's counselor said that his urine number showed
he was making remarkable progress. The results had been especially
good, Camery was told, while he had been fasting.

::

At the time the Colonel was being treated, there were about
twenty inpatients at Murrieta, most of whom were older women.
Some of them spoke about the highly unconventional medical
treatments they had been advised to undertake. One elderly
woman from Mexico City had painful arthritis and had been told
to stop her medication during her fast. Two young women with
diabetes left the program early, after it was suggested that they
gradually eliminate their insulin.

What was especially striking about the place was that there was
more talk around Murrieta's well-groomed grounds about making
money than about curing people. The Colonel's Rolls-Royce had
the desired effect right away. As soon as Dr. Horace Gibson saw it,
he told Camery to talk to Dr. Rudd about investment opportunities at the spa, saying, "We can always use a few million."

The Colonel quickly arranged a meeting with Dr. Rudd and
an associate. Dr. Rudd, sitting casually outdoors and unaware
that he was being recorded, told Camery that some money would
be a big help, especially as he was presently waiting for a loan to
go through. He tantalized his guests not with the spa's medical
mission but with the remarkable tax shelters it could afford. "It's

just unreal what you can do in the field of taxes if you know how to use one of those foundations," Rudd said.

::

The Colonel and his cohorts had been at the spa for nine days when Mike Wallace decided it was time he went to see Dr. Rudd

---

THE ROAD MORE TRAVELED

Over the years, *60 Minutes* correspondents have been offered opportunities to invest in all sorts of scams. Steve Kroft went undercover to talk to Bill Whitlow, who had a thriving business rolling back odometers on used cars and forging their titles, all to increase resale value. Kroft posed as a potential investor who might want to put $100,000 into the operation.

Whitlow was very forthcoming, saying that in an average month he might make $50,000 tax free. Whitlow said he hadn't filed taxes for thirteen or fifteen years. When Kroft told Bill Whitlow he had the whole thing on tape, he had a good news–bad news scenario for him. "The good news is we're not cops," Kroft said. "The bad news is we're *60 Minutes.*"

As a result of the program, Whitlow got seven years in a federal penitentiary. Steve Kroft said he felt a little sorry for Bill Whitlow because people can get just six months in a more comfortable "Club Fed" for much more serious offenses. For his part, Whitlow blamed the reporter for his predicament. "You can scrape the bottom of hell with a fine-tooth comb," he said, "and never come up with a man like Steve Kroft."

himself, as an out-in-the-open *60 Minutes* reporter. Rudd had no idea that Goldin, Cook, and Camery had any association with Wallace who arrived with a separate camera crew.

There was an underlying atmosphere of commerce that seemed to pervade Murrieta. This atmosphere prompted Mike Wallace to begin by asking Rudd whether he was in the health care business or the real estate business. Standing on a nicely maintained putting green, Rudd responded that he had to be in the real estate business to stay in the health care business. Not everything in this apothecary's garden was rosy. Rudd did concede that he had some cash-flow problems and that the interference of the local sheriff had slowed him down somewhat.

Rudd was a somewhat short, unremarkable-looking man with combed-back graying hair. He served as the promoter of the Murrieta Health Clinic, but he was also a self-described Baptist minister who preached each Sunday at the Murrieta Chapel. Mike Wallace wanted to know about his seemingly impressive credentials. Rudd admitted he was not a medical doctor. But he did have two Ph.D.'s. Wallace asked him what they were in, eliciting a somewhat confused response:

R. J. Rudd: "In economics and one in philosophy. And I also am
a—a—a full-time licensed ordained minister of the
Gospel. My two Ph.D.'s, one came from the Tennessee
University, and from a—"
Mike Wallace: "University of Tennessee?"
Rudd: "No, the Christian Tennessee University. And I got one
from Florida—Te—Tennessee— Let's see. Trinity
Christian College in Florida."

Wallace noticed that Rudd had his diplomas on display on the wall in his office. The two men, trailed by the camera crew, went over to look. Rudd said that he believed Trinity Christian College was presently in Fort Lauderdale, Florida, but Wallace noticed that Rudd's Trinity Christian diploma had been signed and sealed in Brownsville, Texas, in 1973. Tennessee Christian was near Chattanooga, Rudd said, although he didn't sound too sure.

FALSE DIAGNOSIS

Over the years, *60 Minutes* has reported on other kinds of fake degrees. In 1985, Diane Sawyer reported on the practice of selling phony medical school diplomas. She met an agent for the U.S. Postal Service who had bought a medical degree over the phone. It was easy, if pricey. All the agent had had to do was pay $16,500 and fly to the Dominican Republic to pick up her diploma at graduation time from the school, CETECH. That investigation led to the arrest of the degree peddler, thirty of his clients, and other instant doctors who had been practicing medicine in states from New York to Texas.

Diane Sawyer met one man who had managed to work for ten years in various civilian and military hospitals, including Bethesda Naval Hospital, without any legitimate license whatsoever. He had attended at hundreds of operations over the years as an anesthesiologist. How widespread was this phenomenon? Dr. Pascal Imperato, who had run the Health and Hospitals Corporation in New York City, told Sawyer about "offshore medical schools" like CETECH. He reckoned, in 1985, that there were "several thousand" physicians with fraudulent diplomas practicing in the United States.

Authorities in Tennessee, Florida, and Texas later said that what Rudd had on his wall were mail-order degrees from nonexistent universities. Church officials had also denied many times that Rudd had ever been ordained a Baptist minister.

::

The Murrieta testing lab had an aura of medical professionalism about it, with rows of measuring tubes arranged in lines being worked by a technician. There, Mike Wallace asked Dr. Horace Gibson about his medical methods. Gibson admitted he didn't test every patient's blood or give everyone an X ray. He could get a blood test done if he needed to, but it was not routine. When Gibson was asked what he did when he examined someone, Gibson said he used his "forty years of experience, Mike, just like you use yours in your work."

Wallace was also curious about some of the health products being promoted hard at the spa. They were products with names such as "Mivita," "Fo-Ti-Tieng," and "Formula-X." Wallace asked Gibson what Mivita was for.

Horace Gibson: "Well, it's good for wounds—wounds externally."
Mike Wallace: "Well, wait a minute. I've taken a look at that bottle of Mivita, and it says drink it."
Gibson: "You can drink it."
Wallace: "You can drink it. You can use it for a douche. You can use it for an enema. It's good for hemorrhoids. All these things?"
Gibson: "Hm-mmm."

Dr. Horace Gibson

An independent toxicologist and chemist who analyzed the Murrieta products without knowing what they were being peddled as said that Mivita, which sold for $6 a quart, was "a very small amount of material and a lot of water." Fo-Ti-Tieng was a kind of tea that cost $13.50 for fifty capsules, and Formula-X was, essentially, rubbing alcohol. At the time, rubbing alcohol cost nineteen cents a quart in a drugstore, while Formula-X was being sold at $12 for three ounces.

Mike Wallace wanted to know if Dr. Gibson was ashamed to be part of an operation that sold rubbing alcohol at such an enormous markup. By this point, Dr. Gibson was looking more and more uncomfortable. He said he thought they should eliminate it. Dr. Rudd, who was sitting next to Gibson as he was trying to deal with Wallace's questions, said he hadn't known they were even using it.

::

R. J. Rudd had big expansion plans for his spa operation. He told Mike Wallace that he wanted to build 350 Murrieta-like facilities across the country. Also, his treatment was being promoted by a national network of at least eight hundred "testers." Many of these individuals had paid Rudd $1,500 for one week's tuition at Murrieta. They sent him a commission on urine and saliva tests they performed when they got home and also referred their clients to Rudd for further treatment. Murrieta was being franchised.

Many of the therapies were extraordinarily expensive. Rudd admitted that a urine test could cost more than $2,000. He also confirmed that he projected a long-range business plan that had four thousand testers doing as many as forty thousand procedures a day for a gross of $400,000. Mike Wallace knew those figures because they were ones that had been used on the Colonel by Rudd as part of his sales pitch. When he was asked about the much-vaunted computer that analyzed all the urine and saliva tests, Rudd said that it was set up somewhere in California, in the Los Angeles area, but he was vague as to exactly where. Apparently it wasn't available for inspection at that precise moment.

::

Finally, the Colonel, his nephew, and his secretary revealed themselves to be *60 Minutes* staff. This scene, enacted outdoors in a very civilized manner, attracted a small crowd of onlookers. Wallace asked Dr. Gibson about his initial, brief, and particularly emphatic evaluation of the Colonel. Gibson admitted that no, it wasn't possible to tell if someone had leukemia simply by looking into his eyes. But Dr. Gibson had told Camery he didn't have leukemia without looking at his medical records or performing any more sophisticated tests, either. Gibson said that as far as he knew Camery didn't have leukemia. He didn't seem to be able to remember precisely what he'd said to the Colonel when he'd examined him.

Mike Wallace next produced Camery's "urine-saliva" analyses and told Gibson that he had unwittingly tested Greg Cook's and Marion Goldin's urine when he'd thought he was working with the Colonel's alone. "These don't mean anything as they are, they're just a bunch of mixed-up specimens," said Gibson, looking at the numbers. No one had thought to tell the Colonel that at the time. And claiming that numbers varied greatly during a fast, as Gibson tried to do, was no help because Camery had never actually been fasting. Dr. Rudd gamely stood up for his testing methods. It was still his opinion, he said, that the tests could evaluate changes in an individual's body chemistry.

Moving on to some of the other unusual treatments offered at Murrieta, Wallace mentioned a woman he'd spoken with who had been enrolled for two to three months and been given twenty-four colonic irrigations over that period. When asked if he thought that was medically a good idea, Gibson admitted that it "may be a little excessive." There was also the case of another elderly woman who had been placed on an eight-day fast. In the light of everything he'd observed, Wallace asked Rudd a couple of direct questions.

Mike Wallace: "The question is, are you preying on human frailty? Preying on the elderly? On the abandoned? Taking money from people who can't afford to give that money in order to try to build yourself some kind of small empire?"

R. J. Rudd: "I don't believe that's true."

Wallace: Many who disagree with you would say there's a kind of con-game operation going on at Murrieta Springs right now. They're not delivering what people are paying for."

Rudd: "Well, I still feel this is not a con game. I feel it's a sincere effort by a lot of good people who are giving some of the best years of their life here to—to build a retreat program where people can come and get nutritional assistance."

Rudd with Wallace

In the crowd, watching Rudd defend himself, was local doctor Michael Perlin. He was appalled by what he heard. In telling people to stop taking their insulin, the staff at Murrieta was, in effect, practicing medicine without a license. Urine analysis, on which the whole treatment was based, was a limited medical tool. "I don't know how you can make a diagnosis on numbers that don't mean anything," Dr. Perlin said.

Rudd did have his passionate defenders. Such as his young secretary, Halina Allain, who said that detractors shouldn't just look at the "little things." You could kill any hospital or doctor, she contended, by concentrating on the little things.

Halina Allain's own sister-in-law Stella offered a different perspective. In a letter, she accused Rudd of bilking her out of her life savings of $5,000. Rudd needed the money, he had said, for his computer. In exchange, he had given Stella a handwritten receipt and promised to give the money back in a month with interest. More than six months later, she had seen nothing.

Another woman, Helene Senay, had lent Rudd $200,000 and was wondering what had become of it. She didn't know if it had disappeared into a hole or if someone was building a nest egg out of it. Mike Wallace asked Helene Senay if she was talking to the FBI about all this. Senay said it was talking to her. The FBI had come calling at eight o'clock one morning. As she said, "You usually open the door when they knock."

It had become clear that Murrieta was only one of a number of costly enterprises R. J. Rudd had a hand in. Mike Wallace asked Rudd about a newspaper report of a securities charge in Florida that had led to his arrest. The report alleged that an elderly leukemia victim had lost $25,000 in a land investment scheme. Rudd told Wallace that there had been an investigation into that but that the findings had been news to him. He said there'd never been a trial on it and his own attorneys were checking on the investigation.

Golden Zimmerly, the elderly woman in question, had no doubts about Rudd. "I think he's a con man," she said. Zimmerly, who also suffered with crippling arthritis, had been introduced to Rudd in Cocoa, Florida, in 1973. She had given Rudd $25,000 with only a handwritten contract as security. A number of R. J. Rudd's victims might well have seconded her closing comments:

Golden Zimmerly: "I never thought a Baptist minister, or any kind of minister, would cheat you out of your money. I didn't know they were that crooked, but I found out that they are. That is, if he *is* a minister."

Executive producer Don Hewitt remembered Rudd on a special edition of the program dedicated to the con men the program has encountered over the years. On occasion, Hewitt said, he had felt sorry for some of the scam artists it had exposed. But not R. J. Rudd. "This was such a patently phony and dangerous racket that I had no second thoughts about doing that story," he recalled. Mike Wallace agreed: "This was a bold, bold, mean-spirited scam," he said.

Mail-Order Ministers

:: September 26, 1976 ::

Some people display a remarkable resourcefulness when it comes to turning up ways to legally reduce their tax liabilities. In 1976, Morley Safer investigated a method thousands of Americans had discovered that allowed them to pay no taxes at all. Or so they believed. These people were becoming men and women of the cloth, and they were doing it for little more than the cost of a postage stamp.

Federal and local tax laws allow deductions for churches and clergy. Morley Safer found that thousands of people—Jews, Catholics, and Protestants alike—were embracing a second religion in order to take advantage of tax concessions. The converts included half the town of Hardenburgh in upstate New York. They had become, en masse, ministers of the Universal Life Church as a tax protest.

Bishop Kirby Hensley

In 1976, Universal Life was the fastest-growing church in the country. It boasted a membership of no fewer than five million. Many had joined simply to earn the reward of the clerical tax exemption, although others viewed their association with the church as a spiritual relationship, not just a marriage of convenience. Universal Life had also issued charters to fifteen thousand churches, and its newspaper had a hundred thousand subscribers. Its main business, however, was issuing credentials.

To join the church, and thus to become a preacher or even a bishop, all someone had to do was write in to ask for the relevant documentation. The church would send back credentials without charge, although it wouldn't refuse what was described as a "goodwill offering." A Doctorate of Divinity, however, cost twenty dollars and was guaranteed to be as valid as the Reverend Dr. Billy Graham's.

For just two dollars a month, anyone could start his own branch of the Universal Life Church. Universal Life–chartered services looked for all the world like more traditional religious gatherings. In Orange County, California, for example, Drs. Mary and Jack Lee presided over a service complete with hymns, prayers, and sermons. The Lees were mail-order Doctors of Divinity and ministers of Universal Life. Jack Lee read a passage from the Bible for the program, unfortunately stumbling over the word "firmament."

The Reverend Hugh Biggs, the marrying minister of Niles, Michigan, was another mail-order alumnus. On the strength of his diploma from the Universal Life Church, Reverend Biggs was marrying couples every half hour the night *60 Minutes* paid a visit. Morley Safer also followed Margaret Clement on her rounds in Glendora, California. For twenty dollars, she had become the Reverend Dr. Margaret Clement and operated a Spiritual Guidance Center, offering faith healing on her house calls.

::

Why is the Universal Life Church included among this pack of con artists from the annals of *60 Minutes*? Who said it was a con? The Universal Life Church was set up in Modesto, California, by Kirby Hensley, a man Morley Safer described as an "illiterate ex–Holy Roller preacher." *60 Minutes* visited services performed by some of Hensley's graduates, and clearly some of these people took their ministerships very seriously. But this is what Hensley, the founder of the Universal Life Church and the self-proclaimed "Modesto Messiah," told Morley Safer:

Kirby Hensley: "I'm a con man. [*Laughs*] Every other fellow that I come in contact with is a con man. When I give a fel-

low an Honorary Doctor of Divinity, it's just a little
piece of paper. And it ain't worth anything, you know,
under God's mighty green earth—you know what I
mean?—as far as value."

Kirby Hensley was an exuberant man who gave a great interview,
throwing off homespun one-liners in his slightly high-pitched
voice. The Modesto Messiah's very temporal mission was to
make every American a tax-exempt minister. According to Hensley, anyone setting up a church would automatically become tax-
exempt, provided he had a church charter. And he was very happy
to provide anyone with one of those. Anyone could procure a
charter simply by writing to him in Modesto and asking for one.
Then he or she was in business.

Morley Safer talked to a man named Martin Gallatin who
was in the process of establishing a church in New York City
under the auspices of the ULC. Gallatin called it the Church of
Personal Development. Gallatin said that his purpose was part
spiritual and part financial. Gallatin described how he was setting
up his church. His attorney was drawing up papers to set up a
religious nonprofit organization. The papers would go to the
Internal Revenue Service to secure a tax-exempt number. To
qualify, Gallatin said, he would have to show he had people in a
congregation that met regularly. He thought a total congregation
of a dozen or so would do it.

Gallatin said that he presided over meetings each Sunday,
usually around three in the afternoon. The size of the gatherings
was small, perhaps five or six people, but it was limited by the

dimensions of the church meeting place, which was Gallatin's apartment.

The tax benefits Martin Gallatin outlined to Morley Safer were considerable. Gallatin had clearly done his homework. He said a church charter meant he could donate half his salary, and possibly more, to the church. That money would be nontaxable. He could also buy homes or buildings for the church. All of that money would be nontaxable, and the purchaser could have full use of the buildings as long as he was associated with the charter church.

Martin Gallatin: "You could buy a house on Park Avenue, for example, and call it a rectory—and you would pay no state tax or city tax on that building."

Morley Safer: "What about cars?"

Gallatin: "Right. Cars, all your travel expenses. If you have to go to the cathedrals of Europe to travel, to see how other religious groups function, that's all tax-deductible. All your meals are tax-deductible. Everything associated with the church—which can be almost anything."

Morley Safer asked the mercurial Mr. Hensley whether it was his intention to use his Universal Life Church to make fun of organized religion. He said he wasn't making fun of "them," he was showing them up for what they were. His intention was to put them out of business. "I think that they're all wrong, and I think they're wet!" he exclaimed.

Kirby Hensley: "I think they cause more grief and hell upon this
earth than anybody else, as a church, you see, for six
thousand years almost. I don't believe anybody should
get a free ride. We all should pay taxes. If you can get
these other churches, the Baptists and the Catholics, to
pay ten percent, I'll pay twenty percent."

According to Hensley, it wasn't fair that the regular white-collar
worker, whom he called the "little man," was the one who was
actually paying taxes when so many others weren't. The whole
scheme, to his mind, was actually a protest against the churches'
tax-exempt status, not an exploitation of it.

The fact was, however, that despite Kirby Hensley's own tax
exemption for the church in Modesto, there was some question
about whether the same benefit could be applied to the thousands
of other chartered Universal Life churches. Hensley's lawyer,
Peter Stromer, told Safer that the IRS was saying that the ULC
had never applied for a group exemption to cover all the churches.
Stromer said that it was Hensley's position that the thousands of
chartered churches were but one church.

Hensley vehemently concurred: "There ain't no such thing as
a branch church." Hensley said he used the Bible as his guide.
That was what he went by, and according to Hensley, the Bible
said the church was "like a body with many members."

Morley Safer: "Just a minute! You say you go by the Bible, Mr.
Hensley, Reverend Hensley. And yet you spent the
morning knocking the Bible."

Kirby Hensley: "Now, I told you that I done like all the rest of
them, and I—I go back and get what I wanted. Isn't that
what I told you? That this is what I want. You see what I
mean? Now, I go get—if I need a two-by-four, I go to
that lumberyard and get it."

Every church in the country did the same, he said. They'd look at
the Bible and find something they wanted. Other churches would
say, "Oh, that don't mean that there." And "You may have put a
different interpretation. *This* is what it means." "I'm just as big a
crook as any of them is," he said in reference to these "other"
churches.

Perhaps Hensley was beginning to sound a little sanctimo-
nious. Morley Safer said that Hensley's own paper, *Universal Life,*
made a great deal of the issue of tax exemption. And the paper
included a lot of advertisements that were, as Safer put it carefully, "Kind of dubious—slightly, you know, con man—." It was at
this point that Kirby Hensley told Morley Safer he considered
himself a con man. He preferred to believe that it's what you do
and how you treat your fellowman that count.

Hensley conceded that he knew someone was advertising
doctorates in his paper for $250. He wondered who would be stu-
pid enough to pay $250 when they could get one from him for
twenty bucks.

Peter Stromer told Morley Safer that such august theologians
as the Reverend Dr. Billy Graham were honorary Doctors of
Divinity. Stromer said that people of distinguished reputations
had doctorates with the same value as any similar piece of paper

given out by the Reverend Hensley (that is, none) and went around calling themselves "Doctor."

While Kirby Hensley managed to approach this topic with great levity, Morley Safer found someone who didn't find the Universal Life Church amusing at all: Donald Alexander of the IRS.

Donald Alexander: "We think we know the difference between a church and something that's completely phony. We do find trouble anticipating that difference, and we certainly don't have any business inquiring into the validity or lack of validity of the tenets of what is actually a church, as contrasted with a charade."

Alexander then said that people who believed they were rendering their income tax-exempt by sending Kirby Hensley $2 a month and gathering three people in their garage on a Sunday were being misled. Alexander went on to dispute that there were several thousand chartered churches under the auspices of the Universal Life Church, and he refuted Hensley's contention that when he had won tax-exempt status, each and every Universal Life Church had been awarded it at the same time.

::

Morley Safer watched Mr. and Mrs. Hensley enjoy the best part of their day, the 11:00 A.M. mail call. That was when they looked at all their correspondence and counted the money coming in. Mr. Hensley might not have been able to read the letters, but he certainly was able to count the cash and checks. On camera, he was very excited to get his first two-dollar bill. Mrs. Hensley read a letter from someone who wanted to be ordained a Buddhist minister, a Baptist minister, a Catholic priest, or all three. The Reverend Hensley thought he could put that person down for ten dollars.

Hensley with his wife, opening mail orders

Hensley was predictably evasive when he was asked how much money the church was making him. "Well, if you got that out of me," he said, "you'd be the first that's been trying for a long time." The IRS believed one thing, he said, and people around Modesto thought he was the wealthiest man in town. He wasn't that, he said, and he would venture only so far as to say the operation was running in the black. Morley Safer floated a number toward Hensley. "A million dollars," Safer said, to which Hensley replied, "I ain't gonna say, I tell ya."

In the end, Hensley said he wanted people to get off his back. He needed to have a little room to do his thing. And what was his "thing"?

Kirby Hensley: "Make everybody a minister—until everybody
sees a preacher and they get sick of them. They'll just get
sick of them. When you say you're a preacher, they'd
slam the door in your face. Everyone, not one kind, but
all kinds."

The Reverend Kirby Hensley died two months before "The Best
of Cons" special aired in May 1999. Lesley Stahl reported that
Hensley's son Andre was now presiding over the flock, which
numbered nineteen million mail-order ministers. And the IRS
problem had been resolved, though it had cost the church close to
$2 million dollars to settle its old tax dispute.

Morley Safer remembered Kirby Hensley:

Morley Safer: He's the kind of—what?—lovable scoundrel that I
think everyone really likes. I certainly liked him. He was
a wonderful character.

By 2002, the ULC Web site claimed "20 million ministers
since 1959." Since the church entered cyberspace, it has become
even easier to become a minister. It is advertised to take just three
minutes online. "100% Legal and Free for Life," it says. "We
Accept Everyone From ALL Faiths, Beliefs, & Religions."

Pyramid

:: May 9, 1999 ::

The business term "network marketing" sounds innocuous enough. Perhaps as many as ten million Americans are engaged in it in one form or another. There are many variations, but the theme is the same. Someone is persuaded by a relative or a friend that he can make money in his spare time. It could be a lot of money, tens of thousands of dollars. All he has to do is pay a few hundred dollars to get started and find two other folks to pay the same amount. When in turn they each find a couple of people, and these people sign up recruits themselves, the money will start rolling in.

Schemes like this can be legitimate. But they can also be devastating con games that bilk innocent or naïve investors of their hard-earned savings. This kind of "network marketing" has a different, more sinister name: pyramid selling.

In May 1999, Mike Wallace looked at the business of Stan Van

Etten, a man the federal government said was running a particularly successful pyramid scheme through his company International Heritage, Inc., or IHI.

::

Stan Van Etten launched IHI in 1995. Within three years, he had
recruited nearly 200,000 people in the United States and Canada
to join his company as sales representatives. They had each paid
about $1,000 to enroll, enticed by packages that offered significant
income and what was described as "unlimited earnings potential."

The recruits were told they'd be making their money selling
high-end luxury goods like Coach leather bags and Callaway golf
clubs. They wouldn't be going door to door, but would be working
in the living rooms of their friends and neighbors. And they could
also make money by getting these friends and neighbors to join
them as IHI sales representatives.

At the height of its success, Van Etten's International Heritage held national conventions that were more like parties than
traditional business meetings. Van Etten, a large, youthful man
with sandy hair and a fair complexion, marched onto the stage to
the theme music from *Rocky*, chanting, "I-H-I." Van Etten played
to the crowd like a preacher at a revivalist meeting, his voice rising
in pitch and volume as he made his boast:

Stan Van Etten: "We have three thousand reps that join the
company every single week, just like you. You're in the
right place at the right time, with the greatest company
that's ever been around."

Van Etten working the IHI crowd

Van Etten punctuated his statement with a whoop, shaking his fists for emphasis. The audience, on every face a smile, stood as one and clapped and cheered.

::

Pat Fellers was one of the IHI network marketers who felt fortunate to be part of what sounded like a great enterprise. She was a schoolteacher in Kansas when she bought into the spiel. Right away, she recruited her three children as well. Ms. Fellers recalled that IHI was sold to her as a good investment for people who wanted to retire and still live a good life and who wanted their children to live a good life, too. The message was messianic: Stan Van Etten promised a whole new lifestyle, freedom from "a standard day-to-day job and the shackles of society."

Another convert was Russ McDaniel, a young chiropractor who closed his practice to recruit for IHI full-time. His patients were sad that he was abandoning his career. But for Mr.

McDaniel too, IHI seemed to offer an opportunity that was too good to resist. McDaniel felt he could set his family up for the rest of their lives with a good two- or three-year run with IHI.

At the time, it didn't matter for recruits like Ms. Fellers and Mr. McDaniel that this was a new venture in a line of business with which they had no experience. People talked about the excitement of the recruitment meetings. All present were confident they could make money with International Heritage.

It quickly became clear that the focus of the recruits' efforts for IHI was to be not on selling luxury goods but rather on signing up new members. Mr. McDaniel says he was told "with a wink" that they needed to sell product but that none of the people he knew in the business actually did.

In truth, the way the company was organized, it was never intended that the sales representatives would sell anything other than IHI itself. Stan Van Etten wanted them to make their money by convincing others to join the company. They would build what IHI in its literature called a Retail Sales Organization (RSO), which would earn them commissions. These commissions would come out of the $1,000 each individual they persuaded to join would cough up. They would also take a percentage of everything these people earned themselves. It looked as if there was a lot of money to be made if everyone succeeded at his job.

Of course, no one was making more money than Stan Van Etten himself. He was highly successful, a financial expert who had reached the pot of gold and who enjoyed all of the trappings of his prosperity. Van Etten was founding partner, president, and

CEO of IHI, and he lived what he called "a life of excellence" in a luxurious home in Raleigh, North Carolina. Van Etten owned a private airplane, and he and his wife sported his-and-hers gold-and-diamond Rolex watches.

Van Etten and his wife during his heyday

Van Etten was billed as a charismatic whiz kid from Wall Street (he was thirty-seven when Mike Wallace talked to him in 1999). IHI advertisements said that Van Etten had worked in investment banking for thirteen years; he had taken part in seventy-seven initial public offerings and raised more than $1 billion in investment capital. He projected an image of tremendous business savvy. It was said he had the experience of running start-ups and a strong background in regulatory issues—the kind of know-how that is reassuring to those less well versed in the ways of the financial world.

This combination of business smarts and personal success lured a lot of people to IHI. Evonne Eckenroth was one of the first investors in the company and sat on its board of directors. After talking to him for four hours straight one time, Eckenroth felt that Van Etten was both a borderline genius and an honorable man, as straight and narrow as they come.

Another investor, Rhonda Porter, described how persuasive Van Etten was. He was better than that; he was positively inspirational. It didn't matter what her background was, he told her, it didn't matter how old she was or what education she had, she could do it. It would work for everybody.

::

By the time of IHI's 1998 convention in New Orleans, the company was riding high. It had signed up a hundred thousand new sales reps in the past year, and the atmosphere among the thousands of delegates was heady—people partied and celebrated. But the party was stopped dead in its tracks. The Securities and Exchange Commission in Washington filed a lawsuit against Stan Van Etten and described IHI as "one of the biggest pyramid schemes the commission had ever seen."

The SEC charged that IHI had violated federal securities law by misrepresenting itself as a retail business that sold merchandise when, in reality, it sold no products to the public. In addition, investors in IHI were never told there was a natural limit to the number of new recruits who could join. The pyramid would inevitably collapse, and the recruits would almost certainly lose their money.

Mike Wallace spoke with Robert Fitzpatrick, an expert on the subject of network marketing and illegal pyramid schemes, who had written a book on the topic called *False Profits: Seeking Financial and Spiritual Deliverance in Multi-Level Marketing and Pyramid Schemes*. He explained that a pyramid takes money from one group of people at the bottom and gives it to the people at the top. Those higher up the pyramid keep getting money as long as the base expands. The fraud arises because the base cannot keep getting bigger forever and it quickly becomes mathematically impossible for new members to make any money.

Robert Fitzpatrick gave an example of a pyramid scheme. He could enlist five people and take their money. If they each recruited five people, the first group would make its money back. But there is a limit. You have to go through only thirteen of these cycles to exceed the total population of the planet. So was International Heritage a pyramid scheme? "No doubt in my mind at all," said Fitzpatrick.

::

The attorney general of North Carolina, Mike Easley, also came to the conclusion that IHI was a con. A full year before the SEC lawsuit, Easley forced IHI and Stan Van Etten to cease operations in his state.

Mike Easley: "He was in the business of bankrupting people, and he was in the business of ruining people's lives, and it was our job to stop him."

Mike Wallace: "Why should the state get involved? If people want to invest money, they're adults, they know where they want to put their money."

Easley: "Part of the state's job is to make certain that people have all the facts, and a pyramid scheme doesn't give them all the facts. If people knew up front what a pyramid scheme does, what it's all about, and that they were ninety-eight percent sure that they were not gonna get anything back, they wouldn't invest in that. That's not

---

THE ALBANIAN PYRAMIDS

If proof were needed of the harm of pyramid schemes, witness what happened in the impoverished eastern European country of Albania over 1996 and 1997. In the aftermath of decades of communism, a fledgling capitalist-style banking system was set up. Alongside legitimate banks, a number of money scams were operated. Depositors were offered extremely high rates of interest on their investments, up to almost 20 percent a month. Under the money-go-round principle that such schemes use, the first investors could be repaid with the contributions of people who put their money in later. But any pyramid scheme is actually insolvent as soon as it is set up, and it works only as long as more people are putting in money.

For a while, the Albanian pyramids grew precipitously, to such an extent that at one time, a full two thirds of the population had money in one or another of them. As the schemes competed for money, the interest rates they paid were raised to as much as 30 percent a month. This looked irresistible until people started trying to take their money out. In the chaos that ensued when they did and investors realized there was no money there, the government was toppled, and as many as two thousand people were killed in rioting.

what they're told. They're told, 'Give us your money and you're gonna be wealthy,' and that's not what's gonna happen."

Investors in IHI didn't only lose the $1,000 or so they first put down to join the scheme. In many cases, they spent thousands of dollars doing what IHI had told them to do: travel from city to city, host meetings, try to convince other people to buy into the dream. Evonne Eckenroth lost everything she put into the company. Rhonda Porter's Form 1099 showed just $600 in income for 1998. And she spent far more than that—perhaps $5,000—on business supplies and trips trying to get recruits for IHI. For her part, Pat Fellers invested $6,000 that she had set aside for her retirement and for her children's college education.

For some of the investors, the feeling of having been had was actually worse than losing the money. Russ McDaniel said he had a lot of friends who had lost money in IHI. When people have bought into a moneymaking scheme like this, the last thing they are going to think is that it is a scam. McDaniel felt he had been conned by what he called "some of the best." When she first heard about IHI, Pat Fellers thought it sounded like a pyramid scheme, but she was talked into joining. Not surprisingly, she came to wish she'd trusted her initial instinct.

::

Stan Van Etten's con apparently began with his own résumé. IHI's recruitment material talked about his years on Wall Street, but it didn't go into details about what he had actually done there.

Most significantly, there was no mention of his employment as a top salesman for the notorious penny stock swindler Robert Brennan, either at First Jersey Securities or at two other firms connected with Brennan.

The fact that Van Etten had spent years pushing penny stocks for companies that were shut down for defrauding investors was not, needless to say, a large part of the IHI sales pitch. What potential recruits did hear about was the billion dollars in venture capital Van Etten had raised; his seventy-seven initial public offerings; the fact that he was a Wall Street whiz kid. Russ McDaniel said he recalled Van Etten being dubbed "the Bill Gates of Wall Street."

Stan Van Etten himself maintained that he was being singled out. He contended that scores of other network marketing concerns operated the same way and it was his past associations that had caused regulators to come after him. Sure, investors hadn't actively been told about First Jersey Securities, but he wasn't trying to hide anything. As far as Van Etten was concerned, IHI was a legitimate multilevel marketing company and he had done nothing wrong, nothing illegal. If the SEC hadn't filed its lawsuit, IHI would have been thriving.

As it was, in the fall of 1998, Van Etten closed down IHI and filed for bankruptcy. In all, people involved in the company lost more than $175 million. Almost everyone who had invested any money lost out, and Van Etten claimed that he, too, had been left out of pocket over the three-year life of the company. That is not what court papers indicated, however. They showed that during the lifetime of IHI, Van Etten had been paid the sum of $6,557,983.

Stan Van Etten: "I assumed most of the risk, I built the company, I put the most money into it, and I intended to profit from that relationship."

Mike Wallace: "Do you have any idea how many homes have been lost because they can't keep up the mortgage payments—"

Van Etten: "Sure. People have all been—"

Wallace: "—or how many marriages have busted up? It's a sad, sad story."

Van Etten: "I started—started out saying that that wears on me daily. It is the death of the company that has caused the pain and the financial loss. It's not Stan Van Etten."

Despite everything that happened with IHI, some of the people who invested in Stan Van Etten's vision kept their faith in the man. Evonne Eckenroth maintained that he would have a following "like you wouldn't believe" if he said he was going to head up another company. In the front rank of those believing in Stan Van Etten, of course, was Stan Van Etten himself. Evonne Eckenroth believed that Van Etten was convinced that he had done nothing wrong. "People that are pathological liars believe themselves."

It is fair to say that opinions about Stan Van Etten are divided. As Evonne Eckenroth had it, "There are so many that still think Stan hung the moon and stars. But then there's those that would like to see him behind bars."

::

In September 2000, Stan Van Etten sold his 96 percent stake in investment firm Mayflower Capital to his three partners. *The Business Journal* of Raleigh/Durham reported Van Etten as saying "One person can only run so many businesses. I am liquidating everything I own and getting out of the deal-making business." He said he wanted to "make an investment in my family."

Van Etten reached a settlement with the Securities and Exchange Commission over IHI. The SEC release read in part: "The Commission's complaint alleged that during the period from in or about April 1995 through March 16, 1998, Van Etten and others offered and sold interests in a multilevel marketing program which, in fact, functioned as a pyramid scheme."

Under part of the agreement, announced in late September 2000, Van Etten agreed to stay away from the securities business for two years. He later said, however, that he had made his decision to sell Mayflower before he came to his agreement with the SEC.

Will the Real Howard Hughes . . .

:: January 16, 1972 ::

Howard Hughes was one of the most enigmatic figures of the twentieth century. The most conventional part of his life was as a businessman who, beginning with the Hughes Tool Company, built a formidable array of corporations. He was also a successful Hollywood producer and a record-setting aviator who designed and flew, albeit briefly, the famous seven hundred-seat wooden flying boat, the *Spruce Goose.*

Over the years, Howard Hughes became a recluse. From the early 1950s, he was not in public circulation much, and by the 1960s, he had vanished entirely. One of the richest people in the world and a major player in Las Vegas real estate, Hughes became the subject of intense speculation in the media, much of it about his allegedly obsessive diet and cleanliness phobias.

In 1971, the publisher McGraw-Hill paid a writer named

Clifford Irving $765,000 for the rights to Howard Hughes's autobiography, which Irving had helped him write. It seemed like a huge coup for Irving, convincing Hughes, who had not been heard from or seen for years, to tell him his unexpurgated life story. The book promised to be a blockbuster.

At the time, *60 Minutes* had been on the air for four years. Executive Producer Don Hewitt remembered the moment in the 1999 special "The Best of Cons." "You've got to realize, Howard Hughes at that time was one of the mysteries of America." He was a billionaire, an adventurer, maybe the most glamorous man in the country, who had abruptly disappeared. This was a huge story and one that *60 Minutes* became very much involved in.

In January 1972, a man claiming to be Howard Hughes took part in a news conference by telephone arranged by the Hughes Tool Company. Hughes spoke to seven reporters, each of whom had met him at some point in his life. He was said to be calling from the Bahamas, and the reporters were gathered in Los Ange-

Wallace covering the Howard Hughes hoax

les. He spoke haltingly. The connection to the first-generation speakerphone was not the best. But the message came through loud and clear.

Voice of Howard Hughes: "I only wish I was still in the movie business, because I don't remember any script as wild or as stretching of the imagination as this yarn has turned out to be."

Vernon Scott, UPI: "I take it, sir, you do not know a man named Clifford Irving, then?"

Hughes: "No. I never saw him. I never even heard of him until a matter of days ago, when this thing first came to my attention."

At that time, the publishers were standing by their decision to publish the book, but the phone conference raised serious questions about the text's authenticity. Clifford Irving appeared on *60 Minutes* to defend himself and the integrity of his book. Irving spoke with Mike Wallace, the beginning of what would be a long association. They met at the home of Irving's attorney, Martin Ackerman. The two men sat in armchairs by the fireplace. Irving, wearing a cardigan, sitting with his legs crossed, gave off an air of calm and self-assurance.

Irving had claimed that the voice on the phone could not belong to Hughes. He said that there were several errors of fact in what had been said, and in any case Hughes wouldn't have been able to sit through a two-and-a-half-hour conversation without interruption because of his physical condition. Irving also produced two letters he said Howard Hughes had written him authorizing him to write the book. Handwriting experts had verified that the handwriting was Hughes's. Irving said that he had met Hughes numerous times over many months in Mexico, Puerto Rico, Florida, and the Bahamas to tape material for the book.

Irving gave Mike Wallace a copy of the manuscript of the autobiography. It was full of intimate details of Hughes's life from his birth in 1905 right up to 1971. There were numerous legends about Hughes in circulation, and Wallace quizzed Irving about what the man himself had apparently chosen to say about some of them. He also asked about the logistics of Irving's publishing arrangement with Hughes.

Irving showed Wallace copies of letters and contracts between himself and Hughes. The first document was a letter dated September 10, 1971, that had set the project into motion. Hughes asked Irving how he planned to write the biography and asked him not to publicize their communication for the time being. Irving also flourished a photocopy of a letter dated the following day that specifically authorized McGraw-Hill "to publish my autobiography from the manuscript in your possession according to the terms and conditions of my letter of agreement with you dated 3/4/71 and the letter of addendum to that agreement dated 9/11/71." Hughes signed it, "Yours truly."

There was some language about other specific agreements that Wallace presumed to be about money. Clifford Irving said that Hughes was being paid for his participation. In fact, he already had been paid, with checks having been cashed with endorsement guaranteed by the Chase Manhattan Bank. Wallace wondered why Hughes, who had two or three or six billion dollars, would want to be paid a paltry few hundred thousand to get his story out. Hughes's holdings were actually worth $2.3 billion, said Irving. That notwithstanding, Hughes felt his life story was worth something. The man also had a certain pride: "Howard Hughes did not get to be a billionaire by giving things away for nothing."

Next Wallace asked whether there had been any witnesses to Irving's meetings with Howard Hughes. Irving said that Dick Susskind, his researcher, had once been sitting in a room with Irving when Hughes showed up early for an appointment. The three men had stood looking at each other until Irving introduced Susskind. Hughes said he supposed Susskind knew who he was. Rather than slipping out of the room, as Irving hoped he'd do at that point, Susskind said he did know who he was and started to offer Hughes his hand. Susskind withdrew it as soon as he recalled Hughes wasn't keen on shaking hands. Clifford Irving laughed slightly as he recalled the moment.

Clifford Irving: "And then, after another moment of awkward silence, Hughes reached into his pocket and pulled out a bag. We still disagree. I say it was a cellophane bag. Susskind says it was a paper bag. And he said to Dick Susskind, 'Have a prune.' And Susskind took a prune and said, 'This is an organic prune, isn't it?' Hughes said 'Yes, yes, how did you know?' He said, 'This is the only kind I eat. All the rest are poison.' And then they were off and running on a discussion of organic foods and vitamins and whatnot, while I stood there like a dummy."

Mike Wallace asked Irving why, if Hughes was such a sick man, was he flying all over the Western Hemisphere to talk about his life for a book? "Who said he was sick?" asked Irving, bristling. Wallace thought he couldn't talk for more than twenty minutes in a taping session. What Irving meant was that Howard Hughes couldn't talk for two and a half hours straight, which didn't mean he couldn't travel. He didn't have to talk if he was traveling. Mike Wallace wanted to know why he hadn't just met Clifford Irving in the Britannia Hotel in Nassau in the Bahamas and have done with it.

The Howard Hughes that Clifford Irving subsequently began to describe sounded like the public perception of the legendarily eccentric recluse. One reason for all the meetings was simply the fact that Hughes liked to travel. But there was also a secrecy factor. The arrangement with Irving stipulated that none of the people in Hughes's own organization would know about their arrangement. There were certain things that people might disapprove of and raise a ruckus over. And anyway, it was his private business, and Hughes was, Irving said, a private man who had only sporadic communication with members of his own organization.

Take Chester Davis, for example. He was the executive vice president of Hughes Tool Company and Hughes's chief counsel, the man who represented his interests in Nevada. Despite his seniority, Davis had never met his boss. According to Irving, he never would. Hughes wasn't interested in meeting him. Mike Wallace thought it was because Hughes didn't like Davis, which was the impression he had gotten from reading the book. Why would he employ the man if he didn't like him? Irving thought that maybe he was a good lawyer. Pointing at Mike Wallace for emphasis, Irving said Wallace was referring to the transcript, not the book. At Hughes's request, certain things had been taken out of the book that had been in the recorded transcripts.

What about the negative information about another Hughes employee, Robert Maheu? Irving said that Hughes had specifically said he wanted the material about Maheu, whom Mike Wallace said he didn't think Hughes liked either, left in the book. Irving said Hughes had fired Maheu, which Maheu was contesting in court in Nevada. Hughes wanted to make clear that he had in fact fired Maheu and that Chester Davis and another man, Bill Gay, represented Hughes's interests in Nevada.

There was something else Irving had written that Mike Wallace wanted to discuss. Hughes was quoted as saying, "Bribery and favors are at the root of the American political system." With that in mind, Wallace asked Irving about the background of a loan that the Hughes Tool Company had made to President Nixon's brother Donald in 1956. (When the story was broadcast, Richard Nixon was in the White House.)

According to Irving, the full story would be in the book, but he could tell Wallace the basics without stealing Howard Hughes's thunder. The book would say that Richard Nixon's brother, who was running a restaurant in California that served "Nixon burgers," had gotten a loan of $205,000. Wallace tried to get Irving to divulge more about this. Irving said that Hughes had been asked for the money. By whom? By a representative, a go-between, said Irving.

If this were all true, what was the quid pro quo? Why would Howard Hughes lend Richard Nixon's brother $205,000 to make some Nixon burgers? Irving said the answer was in the book. Wallace wondered whether something hadn't been "fixed." Clifford Irving said he wasn't going to call Howard Hughes a "fixer," but he would say he was a man who made very careful arrangements to see that he got what he wanted. The loan had never been repaid.

The man said to have been the go-between was Clark Clifford, the onetime secretary of defense, presidential adviser, and big-time Washington lawyer. He later told Wallace that there was "not a grain of truth" to the charge that he had been involved in the Hughes Tool Company loan to Donald Nixon, although his firm had represented the Hughes Company since 1950.

::

Hollywood made up a large part of the Hughes legend. He'd gone there as a producer in the 1920s and made movies such as *Hell's Angels*, which made a star of Jean Harlow, *Scarface*, and *The Outlaw*, which famously featured Jane Russell in a cantilevered bra of Hughes's design. Mike Wallace asked about Hughes's reputation as a ladies' man. Clifford Irving said that Hughes had known all the great actresses—Ava Gardner, Linda Darnell, Katharine Hepburn. Wallace wasn't sure from reading the book whether his relationship with Hepburn had been an affair of the heart or of the head. Irving said he thought it had been both. Hughes respected and liked her very much.

Clifford Irving: "He said, 'She was a very clean woman, used to bathe three or four times a day, and she always told me that I was divine.' He said, 'And I kind of liked that.'"

Mike Wallace: "I understand he has a kind of classification system for the human beings with whom he comes in contact."

Irving: "Yes, he had a system. I'm not sure if he employs it anymore. It was a whole file card. All his friends and associates, anyone who might fly on his plane and meet him, had a classification: A-B-C-D. And that ranged from filthy, moderately dirty, dirty, and moderately clean."

Wallace: "One hears the stories that he has, you know, long hair and long fingernails, and is a pretty decrepit-looking person himself."

Irving: "This is nonsense."

The last time Irving had seen Hughes, Irving said, he'd had about a hundred and forty pounds on his six-foot, three-inch frame. He'd had the good looks of a man who had once been extremely handsome and had dignity in his face.

Mike Wallace: "Does he wear a beard?"

Clifford Irving: "Not a real one."

Wallace: "Not a real one?"

Irving: "What I mean is that he has on occasion worn false beards and false mustaches and wigs."

Irving took on the look of someone who knew he was telling tales out of school. There was in all this what Irving called a "James Bond setup" that was out of the worst spy novel you could ever read. The second time Irving met Hughes, in Puerto Rico, he had suddenly grown a full head of hair. Hughes said it was a wig he had picked up at a five-and-dime for $9.95. He had to watch out, he said, because people were always looking for him. There was a price on his head, and certain people would like to see him out of the way. That was the reason that Hughes used to employ a man to try out his medications before he would take them himself.

The last time Irving had seen Hughes was on December 7, 1971, since which time the telephone conference had taken place with the reporters in which Hughes had denounced the biography. Irving said that he had asked Hughes to get up and speak and call off the dogs. He'd tried the only way he knew to contact him, which was to send a letter to a particular address using code words for identification. Irving assumed he hadn't gotten the letter yet. Irving didn't know why Hughes hadn't surfaced, and he was puzzled and upset that he hadn't. He was distressed by the fact that Hughes didn't feel he could respond. Irving assumed that Hughes was alive.

The segment left a tremendous number of questions unanswered. The key one was whether Clifford Irving was for real. The piece ended like this:

Mike Wallace: "Is the autobiography genuine? I can only say that it is laced with details that one would think only Howard Hughes could know.

"Did Clifford Irving meet with Hughes and tape thirty hours of conversation with him? Or did he come upon the material, the transcripts of Hughes's memoirs, from some other source?

"I just don't know."

The story continued to develop over the following week, and Mike Wallace updated events on Sunday. McGraw-Hill and *Life* magazine, which had initially insisted they were satisfied with the authenticity of the Hughes autobiography, announced they were holding its publication "in abeyance" until they could look further into what had really happened to the money they'd given to Irving to pass along to Hughes.

Irving had said the checks had been deposited in the account of one "H. R. Hughes" in the Swiss Credit Bank in Zurich, and there were copies of the checks to prove it, endorsed by H. R. Hughes and guaranteed by Chase Manhattan Bank. But during the week, the Swiss Credit Bank said the H. R. Hughes account had no connection with the H. R. Hughes of the Hughes Tool Company of Houston.

Mike Wallace reported that on the Saturday before the broadcast, Swiss police had begun looking for a blond, fortyish, German-speaking woman who, according to the bank's records, had opened an account in May 1971 using a Swiss passport made out to someone named Helga R. Hughes. She had deposited 1,000 francs and left, returned three weeks later, and deposited a check for $50,000 from McGraw-Hill, endorsing it "H. R. Hughes" in the presence of a bank officer.

She had gone back some months later and deposited a check for $350,000, again endorsing it in front of a bank officer. The third check, for $250,000, had been mailed in already endorsed by "H. R. Hughes." Almost all the money was withdrawn—by whom, it was not clear. Mike Wallace also reported that the transcripts of the Hughes-Irving interviews included references to a woman named Helga, purported to be the wife of a diplomat in Mexico, with whom Hughes had said he was deeply in love.

In the interim, Mike Wallace reported, Howard Hughes himself had come forward again, or so said his associates. He'd provided handwritten answers to twelve questions and finger-prints on every page, disavowing the alleged autobiography and any knowledge of the man who had claimed he'd spent a hundred hours with him—Clifford Irving. The Hughes Tool Company hired a fingerprint-examining firm, which confirmed that the prints were the same as those on a copy of an FBI security clearance provided for Hughes during the Second World War.

Also made available for examination were Hughes signatures produced by Hughes's company. These could be compared with another set of signatures provided by Clifford Irving's side, copied from its documents. As Mike Wallace said, students of holography or calligraphy or graphology, or other armchair detectives, would surely study these with zest.

In the midst of all this, Clifford Irving, the man at the center of the storm, besieged by reporters, left the country with his wife for their home on the Spanish island of Ibiza. Wallace said that Irving's publishers at McGraw-Hill and *Life* magazine were reported not to be pleased with that particular development, but Irving promised he'd be back soon.

Mike Wallace: "For the time being, McGraw-Hill and *Life* magazine, who have a considerable investment in Clif-ford Irving, Howard Hughes, and a fascinating if explo-sive manuscript whose authenticity is in question, are waiting for word from Zurich and the Swiss police as to just who is the H. R. Hughes who put his—or her—money in the Swiss Credit Bank."

In the face of intense scrutiny, Clifford Irving's world quickly unraveled. The autobiography was proved to be a hoax, a complete fabrication. Helga R. Hughes turned out to be Irving's wife, Edith. Everything Clifford Irving had told Mike Wallace, in all its scrupulous detail, was a lie.

::

That March, Mike Wallace went on the air and replayed some of the highlights of Irving's interview on the program in January. Irving had been so good that Wallace wanted to nominate him for an Emmy for Best Actor of the Year in a Starring Role.

Wallace played some more of the interview. In it, he had wondered aloud whether Irving would have actually had to have met Hughes to write his book. Indignantly, Irving said they'd worked on the manuscript together for six months. Hughes had searched his soul and desperately tried to get to the truth of his own life. Irving had given, as Wallace commented, a remarkable performance.

In addition to the tongue-in-cheek award from *60 Minutes*, *Time* magazine made Irving "Con Man of the Year." Much more seriously, Clifford Irving had to pay back the $765,000 book advance. He was convicted of fraud and served fourteen months in a federal prison.

::

Howard Hughes never denounced Clifford Irving in person, but his phone conference with the seven journalists was enough to derail him. Hughes's answers weren't flawless, but the reporters

---

HITLER'S DIARY

Howard Hughes's autobiography was revealed to be a fake before it was ever published. But in 1983, parts of an even more sensational set of documents did make it to the public before the hoax was uncovered. These were the Hitler Diaries.

The German magazine *Stern* had procured what they believed to be no fewer than sixty-two volumes of diaries kept by Adolf Hitler between the time of his rise to power and 1945, from a man named Dr. Fischer. It was said that the diaries had been smuggled out of East Germany and, through *Stern*'s eager reporter Gerd Heidemann, the magazine had paid almost ten million marks for them. *Stern* lined up publications, notably the London *Sunday Times* and *The New York Times,* to publish with them, and they printed two million copies of the magazine with the first extract.

The diaries were forgeries, however, and they weren't even very convincing. The books and the ink used post-dated the war, and the diary entries repeated previously published inaccuracies about Hitler's life. "Dr. Fischer" turned out to be a forger named Konrad Kujau who had also dabbled in the Fuhrer's artwork. Kujau and Heidemann were both sentenced to more than four years in jail for their pains. Kujau ran for mayor in Stuttgart in 1996 and got 901 votes. He opened a gallery of forgeries in Stuttgart and was arrested again, for making false driver's licenses. Kujau died in 2000.

were convinced that the man they were speaking with was really Howard Hughes. Voiceprint analysis compared the recording of the 1972 tape with one from 1947 and found a match.

If Hughes had never come forward, it's possible that Irving could have pulled his daring stunt off. The detail in the 230,000-word manuscript was extremely convincing. Irving captured Hughes's "voice" brilliantly, and the handwriting forgery was impeccable. Charles Hamilton, author of *Great Forgers and Famous Fakes*, described Irving as "the most audacious forger of this or any century" and said that Irving's imitation of Hughes's style of speech and handwriting had been "diabolically accurate."

The handwriting, which had been added to the margins of the typescript and was in the "letters" Irving brandished, passed inspection by experts hired by *Life* magazine and McGraw-Hill. Irving did not reckon on the ultrareclusive Hughes stepping forward, even if from the remote safety of his sanctuary in the Bahamas.

::

In 1999, twenty-seven years after their first encounter, Mike Wallace sat down with Clifford Irving once again. Wallace told Irving that when they had spoken in 1972, he couldn't figure out for the life of him whether Irving was lying to him or not. Clifford Irving asked Wallace if he'd believed him back then, and Wallace said he rather had. The technicians and camera people had been saying, "He's lying," but Wallace hadn't been persuaded of it at all.

Mike Wallace: "Aren't you ashamed you lied to me so blatantly?"
Clifford Irving: "Yes. I was—I was lying to everybody. You were
no different from anyone else. I was on—on the train of
lies then. I couldn't jump off."

Irving said that he had first come up with his idea when he'd read
in *Newsweek* about Hughes living in isolation in the Bahamas.
He'd figured he had nothing to lose because there was no way
Hughes would come forward. So the phone interview with the
seven reporters put Irving on the defensive. Initially, Irving
refused to do any interviews. He was afraid he wouldn't be able to
maintain the integrity of his fiction under questioning from a
group of reporters or a pro like Mike Wallace.

The reason Irving gave for not doing any interviews was that
Howard Hughes didn't want him talking to anyone. But
McGraw-Hill, which still believed the book was legitimate, said
Irving had to do something. He had to stand up and say his story
was authentic. So the publisher booked him on *60 Minutes* right
after the Super Bowl (Super Bowl VI, incidentally: Dallas 24,
Miami 3). Intensely aware of what was at stake, Irving said his
heart was fluttering when he met Wallace. He clutched his manuscript against his chest for protection.

Irving, for all his protestations of nervousness, looked
extremely relaxed and confident. Wallace replayed the tape of Irving's hilarious prune story. Irving said he'd have believed it if he'd
heard it. He had rehearsed that story and all the others and had
used them successfully on executives at McGraw-Hill and Time-
Life. Irving said he'd been filled with the success of his fairy tale.

Irving

::

Howard Hughes died in 1976. Irving wasn't sure if Howard Hughes had ever seen his performance. He thought the real Hughes would have laughed like hell if he had seen it. *Irving's* Howard would certainly have laughed because he had a great sense of humor.

Irving admitted he had been deflated and ashamed to have been found out to be such a liar. He said it was awful and that he had retreated—right into federal prison. There Irving was hardly a model prisoner, being moved on from two low-security facilities for bad behavior before ending up at Danbury in Connecticut, decidedly not a country club. He got in trouble there, too, and was accused of fomenting a riot and plotting to kill the warden. But Irving said it had worked out well; he'd been "innocent for a change."

In 1999, Clifford Irving was a repentant sixty-eight-year-old author of twelve other books who lived in Mexico and New Mexico. His *Autobiography of Howard Hughes* was just about to be published on the Internet.

Clifford Irving: "I convinced myself that I knew him intimately. You wondered how I could lie so fluently to you. That's because at some level, I believed everything I was telling you. I believed we met. I believed the prune story. I believed I knew his life better than any biographer, because I had imagined it."

Elmyr de Hory

Fake

:: February 6, 1972 ::

In the midst of the Clifford Irving/Howard Hughes saga, when the autobiography's authenticity was being challenged but before the con was uncovered, Mike Wallace investigated another of Irving's books, one that had already been published. It was called, perhaps appropriately, *Fake*.

Fake was the story of master art forger Elmyr de Hory, who'd made millions of dollars fabricating paintings by artists such as Picasso, Modigliani, and Matisse. Irving said he'd sent Howard Hughes a copy of *Fake*, that Hughes had written back to say he'd liked it, and that the relationship between the two men had taken off from there, leading to the book contract.

In the light of the allegations about Irving's Hughes book, Mike Wallace asked him about Elmyr de Hory. Irving denied that his book on de Hory, which included a lot of details about how to commit forgery, had been a blueprint or pilot project for his own effort.

Elmyr de Hory

60 Minutes acquired a documentary about Elmyr de Hory that had been made on the island of Ibiza in 1969. Prominently featured in the film was Clifford Irving. De Hory was one of a number of art forgers investigated by the program, but he was the only one whose work intersected so neatly with that of another subject of the program's attention.

::

Elmyr de Hory was an artist who would have liked to make his name selling his own works. When he tried to sell his landscapes and nudes to Paris galleries, Irving said, they declined. De Hory began to do simple fake Picassos that he'd sell for about $100. He got more ambitious, and more expensive. He eventually sold about a thousand works over twenty years.

Irving met de Hory on Ibiza and was dazzled by him. In the documentary, he described how he had asked Elmyr to do three drawings—two Matisses and a Modigliani—which the artist had run up before lunch. De Hory added a coffee stain to the edge of the Modigliani to add Paris-café verisimilitude.

Irving then took the drawings to the Museum of Modern Art and said he'd inherited them from an aunt in France he'd never met. In a clever and cheeky aside, he said he'd heard so much about fake art that before he sold them, he wanted to verify that they were genuine. The museum said the drawings were the real thing and couldn't believe he wanted to sell them.

Unlike Howard Hughes, the other party in this Clifford Irving story was available to give his version. When asked about the drawings, Elmyr de Hory said that Irving had pretended he'd destroyed them. His agreement with Irving was that he'd bring the drawings back, but de Hory thought Irving had them hidden away, stashed in a bank vault that could be unwrapped in fifteen years. He didn't picture Clifford Irving as a man who would destroy something for which he'd been offered $15,000, which was what de Hory implied the museum had said they would pay. De Hory was laughing as he spoke about the drawings. When he said he was only mildly surprised he hadn't gotten the drawings back, he must have meant it.

The *Fake* story footage was full of unintended irony. Irving said he had very mixed feelings about de Hory. He found him charming and lovable, but he had developed fictions about his life. If you were to suggest to de Hory that he'd cheated people, he'd be horrified. Clifford Irving said that in de Hory's mind, truth and fiction were intertwined.

::

Elmyr de Hory spoke about his approach to his art. He said he never made direct copies; his Matisses were versions of real Matisses. He described how he would adapt his technique to paint *like* Matisse. De Hory sounded proud of what he was able to accomplish.

Elmyr de Hory: "I made some Picasso without any trouble, and I sold them. As a matter of fact, as far as I know, one of the dealers went to Picasso for authentication, and asked, 'Is that painting your painting?' He said, 'How much you pay?' He said a hundred thousand dollars. 'Then it must be. I'm sure it's by me if you paid that much for it.'" [*Laughs*]

Irving said it would be difficult to put de Hory behind bars because a case against him would be so hard to prove. French police said they'd have to have two witnesses who had seen him paint a "Picasso" and sign it as such, and then they'd have to prove he'd known the painting was going to be sold as a genuine Picasso. Also, any court case would bring bad publicity to any art dealer testifying against de Hory.

Irving said de Hory had lived in the United States for twelve years, illegally outstaying his three-month visitor's visa. He moved around constantly. De Hory said that was because he liked a change of scene, to meet new people and see new faces. You never know why people travel, he said. Clifford Irving said he knew—de Hory was trying to avoid the FBI and the police from four different states. He'd go up to Canada or down to Mexico; he'd stay in New York or Miami Beach and jump on a Greyhound bus to Texas when it got too hot for him.

Mike Wallace said that de Hory had lived on the run until he got to Ibiza, where he was convicted and jailed for two months. His sentence had nothing to do with his forgeries but was for "consorting with known homosexuals and criminals." Elmyr de Hory stayed in Ibiza and lived among the community of expatriate artists, writers, and hangers-on that had been dubbed "the Ibiza Mafia." It was a somewhat Bohemian lifestyle with a lot of slow days in the sun and parties at night. Among the other residents was Clifford Irving.

De Hory enjoyed a certain celebrity on the island. The story footage showed him walking through town, dressed artistically in white slacks, a cravat, and a cardigan with a large leather belt strapped rakishly outside. He stopped to say hello to people sitting at pavement cafés and to invite a couple of people to a party the next night.

The footage also showed de Hory demonstrate how he could knock out a "Matisse." He worked quickly on a picture of a sleeping woman. He'd never offered a painting to a museum that

Irving with monkey

hadn't bought it, he said. De Hory also challenged any art expert or dealer to tell the difference between one of his Modiglianis and one of Modigliani's Modiglianis. If they could, he'd give it to the Metropolitan Museum of Art, which could hang it next to other Modiglianis, which were possibly also by him. At another point, de Hory had said he wasn't sorry for Modigliani, he was happy for himself.

Clifford Irving felt that de Hory was out in the open and the world knew who he was and what he'd done. Now that de Hory himself accepted that and could have pride in his prowess as a forger, perhaps he could, as Irving put it, "recapture the personal vision and that personal honesty that he once had and become a fine painter in his own right."

In the meantime, Irving seemed to find pleasure in de Hory's illicit career as it stood. De Hory gave Irving a party for the publication of *Fake*. Irving had picked up a copy of a British paper that included a piece on his friend. He read aloud from the story, which said that de Hory was holding the art world for ransom. The artist, resplendent in a velvet jacket and an enormous bow tie framed by a silver necklace, read along with the aid of a monocle. Later in the party, de Hory happily showed the newspaper to his guests.

Clifford Irving summed up the attitude of the locals to their resident forger. The slight air of strangeness that pervaded the whole story was intensified by the fact that a tiny tame monkey jumped onto and off of Irving's left shoulder during the interview. It turned out, of course, that what Irving said about de Hory might as well have been said about himself.

Clifford Irving: "All the world loves to see the experts and establishment made a fool of. And everyone likes to feel that those who set themselves up as experts are really just as gullible as anybody else. And so Elmyr, as the great faker of the twentieth century, becomes a modern folk hero for the rest of us."

Without commenting at all, Mike Wallace replayed the first two sentences of Irving's pronouncement when the program was broadcast in February 1972. At that point, it wasn't exactly clear yet who was making a fool of whom.

::

The paths of de Hory and Irving continued to cross after Irving was unmasked just a few weeks later. De Hory painted a portrait of Irving that *Time* magazine used for the cover of the issue in which he was named "Con Man of the Year." In 1973, Orson Welles made a mock documentary about Elmyr de Hory called *F for Fake* in which Clifford Irving was featured. According to Welles, "If the lawyers just let us, we can name you one highly respected museum with an important collection of post-Impressionists, every single one of which is painted by Elmyr!"

In 1976, Elmyr de Hory reportedly committed suicide, although there was speculation that he might have faked his own death, too. In addition to the unknown number of misattributed paintings that are de Horys, there is now a steady market in his forgeries, which sell for up to $20,000. But buyer beware; there are reported to be fake de Horys out there, too.

David Stein

The Gentle Art of Forgery

:: March 4, 1973 ::

In 1973, Morley Safer reported on "the gentle art of forgery." The pursuit of impeccable fakes had attracted what he described as "some of the world's most talented scoundrels." Hardly a museum in the world hasn't, in good faith, hung a masterwork actually painted by a great forger. There have been, for example, some very convincing Rembrandts and Botticellis created. And every few years another apparently indisputable *Mona Lisa* turns up.

Safer said that detecting modern forgeries of old masters was now relatively easy because technology could date canvases and pigment and even the dust and soot that forgers used to add the appearance of age to their work. Finding forgeries by painters who had worked at the same time as Rembrandt or Botticelli was far more difficult. The materials were authentic, so it came down to a question of style, and experts could argue about that forever.

::

The hardest to catch was someone who faked twentieth-century paintings, someone like Elmyr de Hory. He could buy the same paper, canvas, and paint that Picasso or Chagall or Matisse had used. Also, it might be argued, you didn't have to be a sophisticated talent to paint like some of the post-Impressionists. As de Hory said himself, a forger's best bet wasn't to produce a copy of a picture someone had already painted but to produce something he *might* have painted—a whole new Chagall, for example.

David Stein

Morley Safer showed some convincing-looking forgeries of works by Matisse, Modigliani, and Chagall that were all the work of one man. According to his Interpol file, he was "Henri Haddad, born Colombes, France; alias Philippe Ducrest, born Dijon; alias Georges Delaunay, born Vienne, France; alias Michel Leroy, born Nice." He was best known as David Stein, born Alexandria, Egypt, who was what Safer called "one of the most charming villains ever to take brush in hand and stroll down the Champs-Élysées and Park Avenue and through the salons of Palm Beach."

When Safer spoke with Stein, or whatever his name was, he was going straight, painting as himself, and signing his own name. He had been busted by one of the people whose work he was forging and had done some jail time in the United States and France. At his home in Paris, Stein painted Safer a "Chagall," something he would have represented as an original gouache by Chagall in the old days. He said he could sell it for $20,000 to $30,000.

THE FORTUNE TELLER

In 1982, Morley Safer demonstrated just how contentious the issue of a painting's authenticity could be. He reported on the debate about the seventeenth-century master Georges de La Tour's *The Fortune Teller,* which the Metropolitan Museum of Art had bought in 1960 for $675,000, and still owns. There are only thirty-five de La Tours in the world, and until 1960, this one was unknown. The Met had bought it privately from an obscure French country house.

Brian Sewell of Christie's in London was the first expert to say he thought it was a fake. He said he'd seen it being hawked around Paris in 1958 and had declared then that it was forged. Sidney Sabin, an art dealer in London, said it was a "criminal forgery," and de La Tour specialist Christopher Wright said he didn't think it could be taken seriously. Wright said the signature didn't match and that whoever had painted it couldn't draw; Sewell said that the hands were like "half a pound of sausages on the end of a pork chop"; and Sabin, that the eyes were all wrong. Diana de Marly of the Courtauld

A quiet-spoken, benign-looking man, Stein told Safer in his slightly accented English how he'd been working for a French newspaper when he decided he wanted to investigate the art-dealing business. He'd done a simple Picasso drawing and gone to a dealer in Paris. As Clifford Irving had done, he said he got it from an aunt. The telling detail he provided was that the aunt had personally known Picasso in the South of France. The dealer bought the drawing for $2,000 without seeing any authenticating paperwork. Stein couldn't believe how easy it had been, and he

in London, an expert on costume, found numerous problems with the dress, including what looked like a zipper on one figure in a picture supposedly painted in the 1630s.

Christopher Wright also pointed out another unsettling attribute: the letters "M-E-R-D-E" inscribed on the painting. As Morley Safer said, it was not unknown for art forgers and art restorers to add a devilish clue or hint about what they thought about the painting. The Met said that it had conducted a series of scientific tests and that X rays proved the painting was genuine. But the museum wouldn't answer questions from Morley Safer about the picture on the record on film. One thing did happen between the filming of the story and the airing of the broadcast. The word "Merde" was removed from the picture with a chemical solvent before it was sent to France for an exhibit. The Met said the word was evidently created by a mischievous restorer and was removed during a cleaning of varnish used during prior restorations.

started fabricating artwork that he was able to sell all over the world.

In the United States alone, Stein had made $857,000. He knew exactly how much, because that's what the investigation into his activities had established. Stein thought that art dealers were so easily fooled because they just wanted to make money and weren't scrupulous about how. If they were suspicious, they'd just close their eyes. The whole art market was like that. Safer asked Stein how much his biggest sale had been for.

David Stein: "There was a painting which was a Chagall oil which went for $84,000—an oil."

Morley Safer: "Where is it now?"

Stein: "Well, I don't know, because actually this painting never came up in the investigation. It was sold in the United States."

Safer: "To whom?"

Stein: "It was sold to a collector by the name of L. D. Cohen."

Safer: "And is it hanging on his walls today?"

Stein: "I don't know."

Morley Safer found L. D. Cohen in Palm Beach, Florida. An art dealer told Safer that Palm Beach was a con man's paradise. The Gold Coast retirees might not know much about art, but they could afford anything that came along and were eager for bargains. When Stein, the seasoned forger, went down to Palm Beach, he quickly found new collector L. D. Cohen.

Sitting amid his art and wearing a flamboyant blue checked jacket with a matching cravat at the open neck of an orange shirt,

David Stein

Cohen looked like a man who enjoyed his wealth. He said that he had taken his money out of the stock market and bought art with it. Though the market had gone down, the art had appreciated.

Cohen told Safer he thought Stein was a genius, "a con man par excellence. He's suave, he's good-looking, he's talented, he has a flair for conversation." He could play Chopin at the piano like a pro. He could toss off a Chagall or a Picasso on a moment's notice. Cohen said Stein had arrived destitute and immediately bought a Rolls-Royce he'd never paid for; set up in an apartment in the best hotel in town, the Colony; and surrounded himself with beautiful women. He was a master showman.

But when Safer asked Cohen about the Chagall, Cohen said he'd never paid that much for a painting in his life, nor had he ever bought a Chagall. He had only one French painting. He had a Dufy, a de Chirico, a Picasso, and a small Chagall sketch that had cost two or three thousand, but nothing that had cost more than eighty thousand dollars. "Maybe some other Cohen, it's a common name," he suggested.

Cohen did say that he thought there were a lot of people who had been taken in by Stein but hadn't reported it. Nobody likes to admit they were conned. "People have an abhorrence to show they were fleeced."

Safer with L. D. Cohen

::

Stein said it had taken him three or four days to paint the Chagall he said he'd sold to Mr. Cohen of Palm Beach. Most of the drawings just took a few hours. When Safer asked him what he thought the painters might think of what he was doing, Stein had told him a story of how Gertrude Stein had lost a little Cézanne painting and was distraught about it. An obliging Pablo Picasso had painted a replacement for her. As Stein said, Picasso's Cézanne was probably in a gallery somewhere, and it was a forgery, too.

::

Stein arrived in the United States with nothing but an armload of paintings. He set himself up in an expensive apartment and gallery on Park Avenue and insinuated himself into the metropolitan art scene, selling his work to well-established New York galleries.

Stein had the misfortune that three of his Chagalls were shown to Marc Chagall himself for authentication by a dealer. Stein was caught and indicted on ninety-seven charges of grand larceny. Apparently Chagall's only comment when he heard what was going on was "Diabolical!" But Madame Chagall asked the dealer how much he'd paid for the pictures. When she heard how little it was, she asked the dealer, "How could you believe they were Chagalls at that price?"

::

None of the galleries that bought Stein's art cared to comment for the program. Stein was scathing about the response of the art world to forgers like him. Galleries weren't anxious to expose fakes, he said, because it would kill their business. Stein said the prices galleries charged were ridiculous. They couldn't be victims in his kind of crime because they made so much money themselves. So he was playing on their greed, Safer suggested, offering them cut-rate Picassos.

Morley Safer had a hard time finding anyone to speak out against David Stein—not the galleries, not any of the people he'd sold paintings to. When the district attorney went to take a David Stein "Chagall" from Ancky Johnson, she refused to give it up. Johnson, a former wife of cosmetics tycoon Charles Revson, told Safer she loved the picture and didn't think it mattered if it was painted by Marc Chagall or David Stein. Her pragmatic attitude was helped by the fact that nobody could tell the difference anyway.

Johnson said she thought that if Stein had had a rich father, he wouldn't have had to resort to forgery. She said Stein just liked to live well, to ride around in a Bentley and live on Park Avenue. He didn't want to take the time to make it on his own. She thought the starving artist wasn't his style.

::

In 1990, Morley Safer reported on the market for "genuine fakes," in other words, copies of famous paintings. At a time when genuine Impressionists and Post-Impressionists were fetching enormous prices at auction—in May of that year van Gogh's *Portrait of Dr. Gachet* was sold to a Japanese buyer for $82.5 million—there was a lively market in copies of paintings by masters like Renoir, van Gogh, Degas, and Cézanne. As Safer pointed out, there is a difference between a copy that is described as such and a fake that might be passed off as an original.

Morley Safer's ruminations in 1990 on the thin line between copies and forgeries caused him to bring up David Stein, seventeen years removed from his appearance on *60 Minutes*. When Safer met up with Stein again, the artist said he was going straight and had been for twenty years. Safer mentioned a contract Stein had made with Adnan Khashoggi, who had recently been known for his involvement in the Iran-Contra affair. Khashoggi commissioned Stein to paint thirty-seven paintings in the manner of Monet, Gauguin, van Gogh, Renoir, Pissarro, Cézanne, and the like and to paint them on old canvas. Stein completed the paintings in 1986, and maintained everything was legal because the client knew who had painted the paintings.

Safer spoke again with British art critic Brian Sewell, who had commented on *The Fortune Teller* some years before. Sewell thought that painting a copy on an old canvas might be of value if someone wanted to pass a picture off as a fake. He added that he thought there could be a problem a hundred years hence with paintings like this. They could be forged, bashed about, and restored, leading to "appalling problems of connoisseurship and curatorship" in the future.

The market for genuine fakes and copies was apparently especially strong in Japan. And the recession that arrived in the early 1990s was good for the copy business. Morley Safer concluded by talking about David Stein. "David Stein," he said. "Well, David Stein is up to something. Just what, we're not quite sure."

In 1993, the London *Mail on Sunday* reported that thirteen fake Picassos that Stein had painted for a movie about the great painter's life had been snatched by the police. Picasso family lawyers had the paintings seized because of fears that the copies might find their way onto the market and depress the value of the originals. The filmmakers wanted the copies to look as authentic as possible and that was where the problem arose. David Stein's copies were too good.

John Drewe and John Myatt

Scam

:: February 27, 2000 ::

In 2000, another prodigious forger was uncovered, this time in London. As with the Stein and de Hory cases, many questions were left unresolved after the perpetrator was caught, and a large number of fakes were presumed to be circulating around the art world. The artist in question, John Myatt, was not the mastermind of this particular operation, nor were his forgeries the best the art world had ever seen. Myatt painted to order for a man who introduced a brilliant twist to the age-old game of art forgery.

John Myatt's boss was neither an artist nor a dealer but a con man named John Drewe. The forgeries Drewe sold were different in that they came along with immaculately recorded and catalogued provenances. Some of this documentation, which to all appearances established the authenticity of the pictures, was fabricated by John Drewe. The supposed provenances of a large number of works, purported to be by masters of twentieth-century art, were thrown into doubt as a result.

It was, said Morley Safer, the art scam of the century. For nine years, art galleries and auction houses in London and New York had bought and sold two hundred fakes supposedly by the likes of Matisse, Braque, Giacometti, Graham Sutherland, and Ben Nicholson. At least a hundred of the artworks hadn't been recovered. There was the now-familiar reticence on the part of members of the art world to look too closely or to try to establish how much damage Drewe and Myatt might have caused.

In 2000, John Drewe was serving six years in Pentonville Prison in London for his role in the affair. Drewe's operation had taken in some of the world's most prestigious art and auction houses, often for very large sums. In one case $180,000 had been paid for one painting. British prisons do not allow cameras, so Drewe wrote a letter to *60 Minutes*. In it, he protested his innocence, claiming he had been a victim of dark forces in the British

John Myatt

government. But for Detective Miki Volpe of Scotland Yard's Art Fraud Unit, who had spent three years on the case, the only dark force involved was Drewe himself, the cleverest and most effective operator his unit had ever encountered.

Drewe hadn't done any of the painting himself; he'd used John Myatt, who had struggled to sell his own stuff before he achieved much greater success faking the work of much better known painters. Myatt was eventually turned in by Drewe's disaffected wife. Detective Volpe said that Myatt was very forthcoming when he was arrested. It was as if he had expected the knock at the door. Myatt cooperated with the police and served just four months in prison. He went back to painting the masters after he got out but took to signing them with his own name.

John Myatt told Morley Safer that his career as a forger had begun in 1986. At the time, he was trying to make a living teaching art. He put an ad in a London satirical magazine offering to paint "genuine fakes" of the masters. Among the responses was an order from John Drewe for a Matisse. Myatt met Drewe at Euston train station in London and handed over the picture, which Drewe said he wanted as a present for his wife. Drewe must have liked what he saw because he ordered more paintings: Braques, Bissières, Le Corbusiers, Giacomettis.

Drewe called Myatt one night and said he'd taken one of Myatt's paintings, a small Cubist rendering, to an auction house. It had valued it at £26,000, around $50,000 at the time. Myatt said he couldn't believe it. He immediately told Drewe he was interested in more of that kind of work. He had two babies to look after at home, and he needed the money. According to Myatt, it didn't actually occur to him that what he was about to get involved with was illegal, something he admitted sounded strange.

::

As Clifford Irving, Elmyr de Hory, and David Stein have all proved, it is possible to sell fake pictures with no more documentation than a good story and a winning manner. Drewe's masterstroke was to go into the archives of major museums to plant authentication of the paintings he was ordering from Myatt. Detective Volpe described how Drewe had ingratiated himself at the Tate Gallery, one of the institutions he penetrated. Drewe had donated £20,000 to the Tate, after which he could plausibly ask to see some of the gallery's archive material. He was given a reader's ticket that he used to move freely about the archives.

Using a period typewriter, old paper, phony rubber stamps, and black-and-white photos of Myatt's pictures, Drewe created histories, bills of sale, and auction prices that he inserted into the files. He also infiltrated the National Art Library at the Victoria and Albert Museum and the Institute of Contemporary Art and went to work in the archives of these establishments, too.

Detective Volpe said that Drewe's fakes were very good. He used an ingenious trick, one that provided ammunition to use in his sales pitches. Drewe would have a buyer come over from New York, for example, and take him to the Tate Gallery, where he would use his reader's card to get into the archives. There he was able to show the potential buyer a provenance he'd made and added to the files for a painting he himself had commissioned from John Myatt.

This elaborate care with the documents did not extend to the execution of the paintings themselves, however. Myatt used quick-drying water-based acrylic paint rather than the oil paints the genuine painters had used. None of the experts noticed that the pictures were made with house paint.

Myatt and Safer

John Drewe's persuasive personality was one reason the con worked as well as it did. Myatt said Drewe was "spellbinding . . . exceptional." He thought that if Drewe had put his talents to something more legitimate, such as "politics or broadcasting," he'd have done extremely well. Drewe claimed to Myatt and others that he was a spy and a nuclear physicist with graduate degrees and big connections.

Myatt felt that Drewe believed what he was saying, even when it came to the phony paintings. He recalled one conversation in which Drewe had been talking about the "Giacometti" and so on. Myatt had become frustrated with it and said, "These are not Giacomettis. They're fakes." Drewe had first told him not to say that, then had said, "No, they're not!"

::

Morley Safer spoke with author and art critic Geraldine Norman about the public fascination with forgers; she echoed a statement of Clifford Irving.

Geraldine Norman: "People love to see authority figures slipping on a banana skin, and there's nothing so good as the— the magnificent director from such-and-such museum who has just been taken in by—by Myatt."

Peter Nahum, a leading London art dealer, admitted he had purchased two works from Drewe. He said he had bought one of them only because someone from Christie's had authenticated it. The second, a "Ben Nicholson," had been sold at Sotheby's in New York in 1994 for $50,000. That painting had been authenticated by the Tate Gallery. The buyer's name hadn't been revealed, and no one had come forward when the artist's true identity was revealed.

Geraldine Norman said that one problem with authenticating art is that experts don't have much faith in themselves. Often, in a questionable case, they're not sure whether the painter was just having a bad day or if the picture is actually a fake.

Morley Safer: "Is that what—really what it's about—about that name in the corner? I mean, even if it's a bad Matisse, it says Matisse or Chagall or Picasso or whatever."

Geraldine Norman: "Absolutely."
Safer: "So it—it has nothing to do with art, it only has to do
          with a kind of trophy?"
Norman: "It's trophy hunting, yes."

Detective Volpe wondered how many of the buyers of the hundred unrecovered paintings would actually surface. Some people
might not like to admit they'd been duped. Police couldn't find any
of Drewe's records that might help with the process, and Myatt
said he hadn't kept any. Peter Nahum thought that quite a few of
the fakes might have ended up in Japan. Wherever they were, they
might possibly be bought and sold as genuine originals.

Morley Safer: "There are paintings out there from your previous
          life that may be changing hands for—for thousands or
          hundreds of thousands of dollars."
John Myatt: "Morley, what can I do about it? What would I do
          if I was concerned about it? What difference would it
          make if I was concerned about it? Answer: Nothing,
          nothing, and none."

Even if someone did come forward with one of the fakes, there
was very little he could do about it. Morley Safer said it seems
that dealers and auction houses cannot be held liable because the
paintings were authenticated by "experts." And because of the
"perfect" provenances.

::

As John Drewe was serving his six-year jail sentence for fraud, *Variety* reported that Michael Douglas had bought the movie rights to an investigative piece about the case. Douglas planned to play Drewe himself. John Myatt also had a brush with show business when he cowrote a song called "Silly Games" for Janet Kay, which was a hit in the United Kingdom in 1979.

1-800-CON MAN

:: September 29, 1991 ::

In 2001, Americans charged $1.3 trillion on credit cards. Bank-issued credit cards alone carried 18 percent of individual consumer spending. If you add store cards and debit cards, that figure rises to almost a quarter. And amid all that business, there is a good deal of fraud. In 1991, Mike Wallace discovered just how easy it is for a con man to run a successful scam using credit cards. All he needs is access to a telephone. Danny Faries, the con man in question, stole as much as $2 million worth of merchandise over the phone, despite the fact that he was an inmate in Miami's Dade County Jail at the time.

Faries was able to operate by taking advantage of the privilege offered prisoners in the Dade County system to make local and toll-free calls from their cells, in his case, first from a large cell, and later, from a six-by-eight-foot cubicle. Danny Faries told Mike

Danny Faries and Mike Wallace

Wallace that his circumstances meant he could give free rein to his imagination.

Danny Faries: "I would challenge you, Mr. Wallace, if they put you in a room the size of your bathroom at home for years at a time with a telephone, that—I would challenge you to—that you would come up with some pretty inventive stuff to do, because you do everything through the phone."

Faries ran a nationwide operation that he called the Jailhouse Shopping Network. Accomplices on the outside would provide Faries with credit card numbers taken from charge slips picked out of hotel Dumpsters. Faries would use his jail-cell phone to order merchandise from mail-order catalogs using the stolen numbers and would have the orders sent by overnight delivery to his cohorts, who would then sell the stuff and split the proceeds with him.

Faries took a telephone he shared with other inmates, kept it in a vacant cell, and used it as his private business line. From the cell he ran his network, doing what he described as a "bumper business." He ordered high-end items such as collectible gold and silver coins, Rolexes, and camcorders. Faries told Mike Wallace that it was easy to find confederates, and he always divided things fifty-fifty with them. Even when one of them stole whatever Faries had ordered from jail, he was able to take it in stride: it wasn't as if he'd paid for it anyway.

Danny Faries didn't just order goods he could resell. He ordered fine champagne, gourmet gift baskets, and thousands of roses and had them sent to the families of his fellow prisoners. He claimed that other beneficiaries of his largesse were his own prison guards.

Danny Faries: "They're working stiffs, you know. They're not making much money, and they're seeing this stuff going on, and they're hearing about Dom Pérignon and trips to the Caribbean, and there I am in my cell. They know what's up. There's not—you know, and I tried to send, at Christmas and on holidays, you know, baskets and—"
Mike Wallace: "And it cost them nothing."
Faries: "Oh, no, no. Perish the thought."

Jail officials denied it, but one investigator told Mike Wallace off camera that he believed certain guards had received items from Danny Faries.

Mike Wallace also asked Danny Faries about claims that he

was stealing money from people to give to charity. He had a piece of correspondence from Save the Children that had been mailed to Daniel Faries at 1151 Northwest 11th Street, Suite 104, his address at the jail. Faries admitted he saw charity appeals on television late at night for sick children in Africa and found them heartbreaking. He'd call in a donation on behalf of someone whose credit card number he'd had stolen. He felt that someone who saw a charge for $22 for Save the Children on his bill would look at the poor children and pay the money. He said that under those circumstances, he'd pay up himself.

Danny Faries came across as an engaging, quick-witted guy whose open face conveyed a kind of knowing charm. But the police didn't see anything remotely amusing or endearing in Mr. Faries or his activities, philanthropic or otherwise. Lieutenant Ross Hughes and Officer Raul Ubieta of the Metro-Dade County police had spent months building a case against Faries, who was already in jail, having confessed to murdering a friend while under the influence of cocaine. Lieutenant Hughes said he thought Faries was "a convicted killer and con man, nothing more." Because Faries was already in jail for murder, possibly facing the electric chair, Hughes said he had no fear of reprisals for what he was doing.

The officers did concede that Faries's self-described "Jailhouse Shopping Network" was very successful and that Faries was comfortable running his enterprise. Indeed, he was allowed to remain in business because Hughes and Ubieta's case was dropped by the Dade County attorney because of what was called "insufficient credible evidence." The officers told officials at the jail what Faries was up to, but they were told it would violate Faries's rights if his phone was taken away. Because he was a prisoner awaiting trial, Faries was allowed telephone privileges.

Mike Wallace: "Listen, you told the correction personnel, 'Go in there and take the phone out of his cell.' What did they tell you?"

Officer Ubieta: "If I recall the memo right, that he couldn't do that."

Jail officials did finally search Faries's cell and took away hundreds of stolen credit card numbers. But Faries still had his phone, and he managed to keep one credit card number, that of a woman named Regina Donovan, that he'd written on the bottom of his bunk for safekeeping. He went right back to business and used the number to pay for a newspaper ad to sell cosmetics and for a telephone answering service. The ad ran in *USA Today:* "Cosmetic package: $89.95 value for only $19.95. All major credit cards accepted." Faries never intended to sell cosmetics, of course. He just wanted a new batch of credit card numbers.

Faries told Mike Wallace how the phone service operators would take the orders and write down the credit card numbers and card expiration dates. He'd check in at the end of the day—by phone from jail, of course—and pick up the card details that had been gleaned from the calls. Pretty soon he had a whole new stack of numbers to work with.

Pete Collins was a freelance writer in Miami putting together a book about Danny Faries and the Jailhouse Shopping Network.

Collins said Faries was working practically around the clock at the time he was talking to him. The network was operating in forty states, utilizing as many as 150 drop sites, and employing dozens of people. In an eleven-month period alone, he may have moved as much as $4 million in stolen goods. How could Pete Collins be so precise? Because the Secret Service told him.

In addition to protecting the president and going after counterfeiters, preventing credit card fraud is under the jurisdiction of the Secret Service. Its agents began investigating the Jailhouse Shopping Network and confiscated more than one thousand card numbers and catalogs in two searches of Faries's cell. Even so, Faries still had access to a telephone and stayed in business. He even posted MasterCard and Visa logos on his cell door.

Mike Wallace: "Everybody knew what you were doing, and you kept on doing it?"

Danny Faries: "It was incredible. I don't know what to say. I just say—"

Faries

Wallace: "I don't get it. Why would they give you access to a
        phone if they knew what you were doing?"
Faries: "I give great phone."
Wallace: "I'm quite serious. Why would they keep letting you
        have access to a telephone?"
Faries: "I don't know. I would—of course, every time that they
        would say, 'If you don't stop this, we're going to take your
        phone away,' I'd say, 'Okay, then, I won't do it anymore.'"

Mike Wallace wanted to find out more about the telephone
arrangements in the Dade County jail. He visited Danny Faries's
office/cell after Faries had vacated it. Providentially for the story,
he walked up and found a man talking on the phone. It seemed as
though it was pretty much business as usual. There was a list of
numbers on the wall of the cell. Mike Wallace called one and
found himself speaking with the L.L. Bean order department. He
sat on the pallet bed in the jail cell and asked L.L. Bean how much
merchandise he could order over the phone. He was told there was
no limit to the amount. L.L. Bean hadn't heard of the Jailhouse
Shopping Network but said that credit card fraud was a problem
for it. It had received an order from a man named Tommie Chappell, the inmate who had inherited Danny Faries's old cell.

Tommie Chappell told Mike Wallace that the phone numbers on the cell wall were Danny's. He was one of a large number
of inmates who'd learned the business from Faries. Faries said the
people he taught didn't have to be particularly intelligent and
only marginally capable. He'd set it up like a train, he said, and

Wallace in Faries's jail cell

almost anyone can drive a train. All anyone had to do was put in the fuel—the card numbers—and the train, which was already on the track, would go.

Chappell wouldn't acknowledge to Mike Wallace that Danny Faries had taught him how to perpetrate credit card fraud. He said he'd never done any of that, raising his hand as if to swear to it. Sergeant Ted Tate of the Metro-Dade credit card squad acknowledged the practice continued but didn't know why. Wallace asked the director of Dade County Corrections, Lonnie Lawrence, who had requested a Secret Service search of Danny Faries's cell, how that could be.

Lawrence said they were legally obliged to provide telephone service. He could take phone privileges away from someone, for example, who called the judge who had put him away and threatened him, but he hadn't been able to confiscate phones from people who used them to scam mail-order companies. Lawrence said

JUST ANOTHER CELL-BLOCK MILLIONAIRE

Lesley Stahl looked into the career of another man who managed to do good business despite the fact that he was in jail. Rayful Edmond III sold $300 million worth of cocaine and crack every year in Washington, D.C. And after he was sent to the federal penitentiary in Lewisburg, Pennsylvania, he sold even more.

Rayful Edmond had struck a deal with authorities by the time he spoke with Lesley Stahl. He had been turned in by a jailhouse informer, and he gave up many members of his operation in turn, mostly to get some consideration in sentencing for members of his family, many of whom were in jail. Edmond was living under an alias in a different jail in a convict version of the Witness Protection Program.

Edmond said he sold cocaine, crack, heroin, and marijuana to his fellow inmates and conducted major cocaine deals on the outside, to the tune of 400 kilos a month, a third more than he moved when he was a free man.

Edmond said it was actually easier to do business from jail. He met the son of a member of the Medellin drug cartel who was conveniently housed in the same prison and went into business with him. Edmond made collect calls from jail and a friend would connect him to Colombia. The calls were recorded but not monitored, and Edmond used code with his phone contacts.

It seemed to be just as easy for Rayful Edmond to do business as it had been for Danny Faries. Edmond once made as many as fifty-nine calls in one afternoon to five states and two countries. Lesley Stahl said that in Edmond's old cell block, where there had been three phones inmates could use every other day, now there were four—that prisoners could use every day.

the jail had been able to restrict the privileges of such offenders. When Mike Wallace pointed out that he had, that very day, been in Danny Faries's old cell, which had toll-free numbers written on the wall, and had called L.L. Bean and placed an order, Lawrence admitted that the system was not perfect.

::

Danny Faries received a five-year sentence for credit card fraud on top of his life term for murder. He was moved from Dade County to the Charlotte Correctional Institution, a much tougher and more restrictive Florida jail. There he said that prison officials made sure that he could no longer ply his trade. "Perish the thought," he said, "that they might think I'm still wielding my telephonic sword." He couldn't do it because the state prison was more sophisticated.

Mike Wallace: "So what you're saying is you're going straight, perforce now, now at Charlotte correctional center."

Danny Faries: "Yeah—or having to go on a new direction, because the—oh, well, I mean, come on. I'm not just going to roll over, Mr. Wallace."

Wallace: "Isn't there a lady in Fort Lauderdale you've been talking to?"

Faries: "I don't know. Who are you—"

Wallace: "Didn't you offer to set her up in business and rent an apartment from her as a drop site?"

Faries: "Oh, I'm sure that I probably did. I've done—"

Wallace: "Recently?"

Faries: "Now, see, you would get a fella in trouble with all these folks standing around here."

With that, Mike Wallace got Danny Faries, despite his protestations, to admit that he had somehow arranged for a woman to rent an apartment.

Mike Wallace: "—where you are ordering or she is ordering or somebody is ordering camcorders and things like this—"

Danny Faries: "'As he nervously takes a drink of his root beer.'" [*Drinks root beer*]

Wallace: "I mean, you're a crook—"

Faries: "Well . . ."

Wallace: "And a murderer."

Faries: "That's what they say. Doggone, I wish they didn't say that, though."

In the year between the first broadcast of a report on Danny Faries and a rebroadcast of the piece, Faries had tried to have his life sentence changed to the death penalty because he felt that if he could donate his organs, he would be more useful. The court turned him down, so he tried, and failed, to kill himself.

As for the phone system, Dade County officials said that they were changing the way it could be accessed. Henceforth inmates could make phone calls, but only through 1-800-COLLECT.

::

Mike Wallace visited Danny Faries again for a broadcast in 1999. Now Faries was serving his life sentence at Lake Correctional Institution in Clermont, Florida. Danny Faries told Wallace that he was high on drugs the first time they had met. "I just smoked a joint," he said, "Just to take the edge off meeting you."

Apparently, that meeting in 1991 had some drastic consequences for Faries. The authorities acted to make sure he couldn't repeat his jailhouse shopping. "I was placed in what they call a close-management situation, which is the hole," Faries told Wallace. He got out of the cell three times a week, to take a shower.

It was at this time that Faries asked for the death sentence so he could donate his organs. Faries conceded he didn't actually want to be put to death, but he was happy for the attention. But when his request was turned down, he did try to kill himself. He cut open his arm, put a garbage bag around the arm, and got into bed. That was going to be, as he put it, "his parting shot," but it didn't work out that way.

After he survived his suicide attempt, Danny Faries was forced into a drug treatment program and he had been clean for more than a year when Mike Wallace saw him. Faries credited his therapist with giving him some straight talking about his addiction and he himself went on to counsel younger inmates. Wallace asked Faries if he ever missed his jailhouse shopping days.

Danny Faries: "I—I have had cellular phones, since we talked, thrown at me like incoming grenades from all kinds of different places. I've been enticed with what you've suggested and I've chosen not to do it, Mr. Wallace."

Mike Wallace: "Why?"

Faries: "Well, maybe—maybe it's self-serving. I have found peace, and—and I don't want to disturb that peace. And it certainly would."

When *60 Minutes* looked back at Danny Faries's story again for the "Best of Cons," Mike Wallace said that he had been "the most likable con man of them all."

Mike Wallace: "The audience loved Danny Faries. Why? Good-natured, let it hang out. What harm was it going to do him, really? He knew that he was in for life anyway."

In 2002, Danny Faries's brother reported that Danny had suffered two strokes in recent years. He had been confined to a wheelchair, but he was doing well enough to get about without one. He'd been moved again, to a correctional institution near West Palm Beach, Florida. Because of his poor health, Faries was in a controlled area of the jail away from the general population and was serving out his life sentence.

The Sting Man

:: April 12, 1981 ::

Is a con still a con if it's run by the good guys? Of all the scams looked at by *60 Minutes,* perhaps the biggest and most elaborate was not instigated by criminals. In the late 1970s, the government, more specifically the FBI, ran a massive sting operation called Abscam to tempt public officials to break the law. Abscam succeeded in netting, among others, one senator, six congressmen, and the mayor of Camden, New Jersey, but it was a highly controversial scheme. It was questioned whether the government should be involved in stings like this at all. And if it was, should it be putting men like Mel Weinberg on the payroll? Weinberg was the key figure in the FBI's efforts, so much so that he was dubbed "the Sting Man" for his part in the scheme. Mel Weinberg was also a convicted con man.

When Mike Wallace delivered his report on Mel Weinberg in April 1981, Abscam was still taking people down. Harrison A. Williams, Jr., the senior senator from New Jersey, was facing nine

Mel Weinberg

charges at the time, including one for bribery. The Sting Man was the chief witness against Williams and all the other politicians. More than that, he thought up Abscam, wrote the scenario, and made the initial approaches to the politicians himself.

Weinberg convinced the FBI to set him up as the business representative of a mythical Arab sheik who wanted to invest in companies in the United States. The story was that the sheik would pay congressmen generously if he could be guaranteed permanent residency in the country. Weinberg, who wanted to help out the FBI with this inventive scheme, was, as Mike Wallace put it, a "confessed swindler." According to one defense attorney, he was a one-man crime wave. Another said that in comparison, the then-ubiquitous J. R. Ewing of *Dallas* looked like Peter Pan.

::

Mike Wallace interviewed Mel Weinberg sitting at a bar. He asked Weinberg if he saw any difference between the FBI investigating a crime that had been committed and setting up and staging one—

what might more commonly be described as entrapment. Weinberg turned the question around and asked Wallace how he'd catch them. "You set a crook to catch a crook," he said. He'd helped put out the honey pot, and the flies had gathered. It wasn't as if he could simply approach a congressman and say, "I want to bribe you." A plausible scenario had to be established; you had to give him a reason. Which was where the story of the sheik came in.

As far as Mel Weinberg was concerned, he was performing a public service.

Mike Wallace: "You've said, 'I'm going to be delighted to let the people of this country know what their politicians are really like.'"

Mel Weinberg: "That's correct."

Wallace: "What are their politicians really like?"

Weinberg: "Well, I personally think they're a bunch of perverts, drunks, and crooks."

Wallace: "Well, conceivably it takes one to know one, you know."

Weinberg: "Well, that's true. No argument there. I'm not a pervert. I may be a crook."

Before his participation in Abscam and his stint working for the FBI, Mel Weinberg ran a phony company called London Investors. He promised loans to people in exchange for a deposit. It was a con: the loans were never paid. The scam was very successful. Pausing to take a puff on his thick cigar, Weinberg told Mike Wallace that London Investors had taken in half a million to a million dollars a year. Weinberg reckoned he had taken in a hundred people a month. He was proficient enough to hoodwink some of them twice, getting some unfortunate individuals to make a second up-front payment. He would say that the first loan had fallen through but there was another bank ready to pick up the loan.

Mike Wallace sounded incredulous. He found it difficult to believe that year after year Weinberg had promised people money and didn't deliver and no harm had come to him. Weinberg recounted one occasion when the uncle of a Miami attorney he'd swindled had come to remonstrate with him. The uncle had wanted to throw Weinberg out of a window and would have if Weinberg had admitted he'd conned the guy's nephew. Weinberg had bluffed, tossing out names of people he knew, hoping one of them would ring a bell. He'd hit the right name just in time; his foot was already being dangled out of the window.

Asked to explain his success, Weinberg said he thought that the people wanted to be taken. As long as he showed off what he described as "the fruit salad"—the limousine, the fancy office, the telex, the phone ringing constantly—potential investors were easily persuaded to commit.

Mike Wallace: "How do you keep the phone ringing all the time?"

Mel Weinberg: "A lot of people calling up wanting to know where their money was." [*Laughs*]

Mike Wallace asked Weinberg whether he had ever been swindled himself. Lots of times, he said. Every con man gets swindled. When Weinberg visited the Yaqui Indians in New Mexico

Weinberg with Wallace

to buy some gold, he felt he should have known something was wrong when he was given a typewritten contract to sign. His thinking, he said, was where would they get a typewriter from? The Yaqui took him for five or ten thousand dollars, he couldn't recall exactly how much. But the irrepressible Weinberg managed to turn this to his advantage by making copies of the contract. He claimed he had sold thirty of them for a thousand dollars apiece.

::

The FBI recruited Weinberg to work for it as part of a deal it made after busting him for one of his swindling schemes. In exchange for going undercover on four cases, Weinberg and an associate stayed out of jail. Each of these cases was completed before Abscam. Weinberg says he continued to work for the FBI not out of fear or even a sense of patriotic duty; he did it strictly for the money.

From March 2, 1978, to December 1980, the FBI paid Weinberg more than $150,000 of taxpayers' money. And in Weinberg's opinion, the haul of corrupt politicians meant the taxpayers got their money's worth.

The first target of Weinberg's Abscam trawl was Camden mayor Angelo Errichetti. Weinberg said he liked Errichetti: "He was something else. He was terrific." If they'd met under different circumstances, Weinberg thought, the two of them could have been partners. Weinberg said he liked the fact that Errichetti was apparently willing to get into all sorts of crooked endeavors: counterfeit money, drug smuggling through the port of Camden, and other such "crazy deals." Errichetti's enthusiasm was accompanied by a directness that Weinberg liked. There was no hedging, no crying, no beating around the bush. The mayor would say what he wanted—and that was to make money.

Errichetti was so keen that he showed up early to a meeting at the Hilton Hotel at New York's Kennedy airport. While Errichetti was talking to Weinberg and an undercover agent in a room, there was a knock at the door. Errichetti opened the door to find an FBI operative standing there. He'd come to set up equipment to tape-record Errichetti, but was now caught red-handed by his quarry. As Weinberg told it, Errichetti looked at the guy, who was standing, speechless, holding listening devices. Weinberg didn't know what to say. But Errichetti never said a word. He trusted his new friends.

It was Mayor Errichetti who led the other politicians to the slaughter. He took Weinberg to a man named Howard Criden. Criden became the middleman who set up the politicians who fell for Abscam.

Mike Wallace asked Weinberg to characterize the congressmen convicted in Abscam. He said he thought the smartest had been John Murphy of New York. Murphy had been extremely careful and suspicious and would never talk directly about money. At a meeting where the shares for the shipping company they were going to buy were being divided up, Weinberg asked Murphy what his share was and Murphy said, "I don't want none." But Weinberg said he had winked, and the wink hadn't been picked up by the camera filming the meeting. Weinberg said if he'd known Murphy was going to wink, they'd have trained the camera on his eyes.

By contrast, Michael "Ozzie" Myers and Raymond Lederer were much less reticent. Myers gave a speech. "Bullshit talks, money walks," he said. He wouldn't shut up, and he wasn't leaving until he had his money. "You," he said at one point, "you're buying me?" He picked up his money and left. Lederer said, "I'm no Boy Scout." He was nervous. When he picked up his money and tried to find the hotel exit, he went left instead of right and had to be steered toward the elevator by Weinberg.

The other easy one—or what he called the dumbest—was Representative Richard Kelly of Florida, who stuffed his pockets with his money and talked pitifully about how poor he was. The surveillance tape of Kelly showed him squeezing wads of notes into various pant and suit pockets. Once he was caught, Weinberg thought he could have come up with something better to say on television than announcing that he had been conducting his own investigation.

Mike Wallace asked Mel Weinberg to talk him through the case of Representative Frank Thompson. Weinberg said that Thompson was an old-time pro, a congressman who talks—but it's double-talk that reveals nothing.

[*From the Abscam tapes*]

Frank Thompson: "There is a very definite extent to which I or any other friendly member of Congress can help them, but it's very difficult—very difficult."

Tony Amoroso [*FBI agent*]: "Well, that's what the money is for, isn't it, is to help keep—?"

Thompson: "Well, I'm not looking for any money."

Having heard Thompson say he didn't want any money, Mike Wallace stopped to ask Weinberg why the FBI hadn't just left the representative alone. The money had been dangled, and Thompson hadn't appeared to take the bait. Weinberg countered that if Frank Thompson had really been an honest congressman, he should have walked out of the meeting himself as soon as the other side mentioned money. Instead of leaving and turning people in, Thompson had sat there and listened to the proposal.

After Frank Thompson left this particular meeting, Agent Amoroso told Howard Criden how he should go after the representative. Judging by the surveillance film, it was a very heated conversation, and Amoroso went after Criden hard. As far as Amoroso was concerned, Thompson wasn't going to say he wanted money if he thought the room was bugged. He was willing to give Criden $50,000 to use to approach Thompson, but Criden was very reluctant, saying that he didn't want to be put into that kind of a spot.

Mel Weinberg was in the room at the time. Mike Wallace asked him if he thought Criden had been browbeaten. He had a relationship with Thompson that the FBI was looking to exploit.

If Thompson could be enticed to accept a bribe, he would thereby be committing a crime. That would give Weinberg and Amoroso a victory because they would have caught a congressman taking money on camera. This might appear to some people to look a lot like entrapment.

Not according to Weinberg. Criden knew what the ground rules were. Weinberg thought he was just trying to be cute when he was protesting to Amoroso about how difficult things were for him. As for Thompson, he came back a second time because of the

---

ABSCAM, CONTINUED

The most prominent casualty of Abscam was long-time New Jersey Senator Harrison A. Williams, who was convicted on nine counts of bribery and conspiracy in 1981. No senator had been expelled from the Senate since the Civil War, so rather than face that ignominy, Williams resigned in 1982. He did gain another distinction of sorts by becoming the first senator to go to jail in eighty years. Harrison Williams died in November 2001.

In 1980, Representative Michael J. Myers of Pennsylvania did get expelled from the House for accepting bribes from Abscam operatives. No House member had been expelled since three Democrats in 1861. The three, one from Kentucky and the others from Missouri, had taken the Confederate side in the Civil War. In July 2002, Representative James A. Traficant, Jr., became the fifth to lose his seat in this way after being convicted on ten counts of bribery, racketeering, and corruption. Traficant was voted out 420–1, his sole supporter being Representative Gary A. Condit of California.

money. He wasn't there to have a drink. It was Tony Amoroso who actually had the tough job. There was a lot of money involved, and he was under a significant amount of pressure.

::

Taking into account the stresses they were under, Mel Weinberg was extremely proud of the job he and Amoroso had done on the congressmen. The two men were relaxed. So relaxed that for half the meetings they weren't properly dressed. Weinberg wasn't wearing socks. The politicians would come to the meetings and talk about how powerful and good they were, and the two of them would laugh along. Weinberg imagined the politicians considering how stupid these guys were while he was sitting there all the time thinking, "You'll get yours!"

Abscam was a government sting operation run by a self-confessed con man. While he was conning people for the feds, Weinberg was careful to play it straight. He sounded proud about how he had played his role. People had tried to catch him in a lie, but they'd failed. "All I do is tell the truth," he said. Weinberg's slate was wiped clean for the help he had provided the FBI. He couldn't be touched.

Mel Weinberg: "I don't do anything wrong now. I became a
          Holy Roller."
Mike Wallace: "I find it difficult to understand how the con-
          gressmen were as, in effect, easy."
Weinberg: "They weren't easy. We were just good."

Joe Meltzer

Sting Within a Sting

:: October 10, 1982 ::

Mike Wallace's acquaintance with the characters of the Abscam sting didn't end with Mel Weinberg. It turned out that Weinberg was not the only unconventional ally the FBI had recruited to ensnare politicians in Abscam. Self-confessed con man Weinberg was scrupulous about staying on the right side of the law while he was working for the feds, but Joe Meltzer, who operated his own sideshow to the Abscam circus, wasn't.

To establish the front for the Abscam operation, the FBI set up a bogus outfit called Abdul Enterprises. This was the entity in whose name large sums of money were offered to a number of congressmen in an apparent influence-peddling arrangement. That was the "scam" in Abscam. Joe Meltzer was employed by the FBI in the early stages of the game and was given Abdul Enterprises stationery by the Bureau as part of his setup. A piece of that letterhead was shown on camera. "Abdul Enterprises, Ltd.," it read. "London—Zurich—Paris—New York."

Joe Meltzer realized that the cover afforded by the FBI could be put to other, more nefarious purposes, and he went freelance. Meltzer used the impressive-looking stationery as part of a scheme to convince twenty businessmen that he could steer Arab loan money their way. What he got in exchange was five to ten thousand dollars in "good-faith money" from each of his marks.

Joe Meltzer

Of course, there were no wealthy Arabs and there was no loan money. Meltzer was running a con, one that netted him around $150,000. What Mike Wallace wanted to know was, while Joe Meltzer had been running his "sting within a sting," using the FBI's good name, had the Bureau known what he was doing?

::

By the time Mike Wallace reported the case, Meltzer was serving fifteen years in prison after being caught and pleading guilty to this scheme. Wallace described Meltzer as "portly," and at the time of his incarceration, he was shown to be a large man with a fleshy face and short hair that was turning gray. He was shown wearing a tan shirt and pants. He had to use a cane to help him walk, and he moved slowly, with a pronounced limp.

Like Mel Weinberg, Meltzer began working for the FBI to avoid a prison sentence—in his case a thirty-month term for another fraud. Meltzer told Mike Wallace that the FBI had set him up in business, paying him $150 a week with car expenses, an office, a telephone, and a secretary—his daughter. The object was supposed to be to lure members of organized crime into the sting that would become famous as Abscam. But Meltzer went well beyond his brief.

Mike Wallace: "In other words, you were working for the FBI,
        but you were also working for Joe Meltzer on the side."
Joe Meltzer: "Yes. That is correct."

Most of the businessmen who signed on with Meltzer came from San Diego. A local man named Scotty Flink innocently agreed to turn up potential borrowers for Meltzer. Flink never got a dime of the finder's fees he had been promised for his work. He showed Wallace the letter Joe Meltzer had used as his bona fides. It was from one Prince Ali Ben Ramon. "To Whom It May Concern," it read. "This is to notify that Mr. Meltzer of Foreign Investor Group is my sole agent for the United States."

Using these credentials, Flink approached some of his business contacts, whom he described as people who needed funding and who saw this as a very good opportunity. These contacts included a Swedish-born financial consultant named Kai Gulve. At the first meeting to discuss possible loans, Gulve was told that Prince Ali Ben Ramon was a son of Kambir Abdul Ramon, who was an emir. His family owned oil wells and had about $400 million handy to invest, with more coming in as oil revenue.

In turn, Gulve persuaded six of his financial clients to sign up. They sent Joe Meltzer a total of $55,000 in good-faith money in advance of loans from the emir's family. Not unreasonably, Gulve asked Meltzer for proof that the loan money was going to be available. No problem, said Meltzer. Just call the Chase Manhattan Bank in New York City, and one of the officers will verify what I've been saying.

It took a while, but when Gulve finally got through to the man in question, he did indeed say that the emir was a wealthy man with at least $400 million on deposit. What Gulve didn't know—and Meltzer did—was that the "Chase officer" was an FBI insider, who, as part of Abscam, had agreed to tell anyone who asked that Abdul Enterprises was on the level. No one from the bank or the FBI office in Washington wanted to talk to Mike Wallace about Joe Meltzer.

::

Mike Wallace set about trying to figure out how much the FBI had known about Meltzer's side scheme and when it had known it. Scotty Flink reckoned it must have known a full year before Abscam broke. When the loan money didn't materialize, he called Abdul Enterprises to find out where it was. Flink spoke with a man who identified himself as John McCloud, and said he was the chairman of Abdul Enterprise's board. In fact, he was an FBI agent.

Flink told Mike Wallace that he'd asked McCloud if he knew Meltzer, and McCloud had said he did. He went on to say they'd done business in the past and were doing business now, although he didn't know if anything was going to come of it or not. But McCloud had done nothing to warn Scotty Flink that he shouldn't be associating with Meltzer.

It was around this time, in December 1978, that some of the promised money was said to have started moving. But none of it went to any of the businessmen. The stall was that the money was now going to come in through the Grand Cayman Islands and not Chase Manhattan in New York.

Joe Meltzer had to placate an increasingly leery Kai Gulve. The money couldn't plausibly be stuck in the Cayman Islands forever. Gulve started getting phone calls from the emir himself, but he was suspicious and taped the conversations. He played the tapes for Mike Wallace.

Mike Wallace: "This is you and the emir?"
Emir: "Like I said before, most of this is being handled by my son Ali and Joe Meltzer."
Kai Gulve: "Right."
Emir: "And, er, I spoke to him about fifteen minutes ago to give him some more information on something else he is working on, because I'm going to London right now, and—"

Wallace: "Well, wait a minute! This fellow doesn't sound any
more like an Arab than you or I."

Gulve: "No."

Wallace: "He—sounds as though, conceivably, he might have
come from—"

Gulve: "Brooklyn is what I said."

The "emir" had made no attempt to disguise his voice. Gulve realized that he and his clients were probably being had. So he
decided to look for help from the authorities. He telephoned
America's most trusted law enforcement agency, the FBI. As he
recalled with a rueful smile, within an hour he got a call himself—
from Joe Meltzer. It seems that as soon as anyone called the FBI
to ask about Meltzer, the FBI promptly let Meltzer know about it.

Gulve taped his conversation with Joe Meltzer, too. Meltzer
claimed he had the FBI under control and told Gulve that the
FBI shouldn't ask too many questions; that it would be in trouble
if it did. He also says he'd called the local head man, "to give him a
little bit of a problem."

Mike Wallace played the same tape for Joe Meltzer in his
prison interview. Meltzer laughed as he listened to it. Wallace
said he had a nerve. But Meltzer said he hadn't really had the FBI
in his pocket, as Wallace said the tape implied; he had just been
trying to fend off Gulve's complaints. Meltzer did, however,
admit he was getting tipped off by the FBI when people called
about him. He would get a call, he said, from FBI agent, Gunnar
Askeland. Askeland would tell Meltzer, and Meltzer would get
back to working the phone, damping down the fires.

Scotty Flink said he had gotten the same treatment when he'd tried to report Meltzer to the authorities. He said he'd received a call from Meltzer six hours after he took a cardboard box full of phony Abdul Enterprise contracts to the FBI. Meltzer had asked him what he had been doing at the Bureau.

Joe Meltzer said that the FBI had never told him to stop what he was doing, although Gunnar Askeland had told him, "You'd better cease and desist; otherwise you're going to end up in jail" every time he saw him or spoke to him. That's all he'd ever said to him. By that, Wallace understood that Gunnar Askeland, and by extension the FBI, had known what Joe Meltzer was up to.

Mike Wallace: "So you think that Gunnar Askeland knew?"
Joe Meltzer: "Oh, I don't think; I know he knew."

Whatever the extent to which the FBI tried to discourage Meltzer from his extracurricular activities, they did nothing to alert his victims to what was happening to them.

A man named Rick Stanzyck was promised a $90 million loan by Meltzer's Arab investors. When he didn't get any money, he tried to do something. In June 1979, he started calling the FBI for help, asking if these people—Meltzer, the sheik, the prince, the emir, all the companies—were for real. Next thing he knew, Stanzyck said, he received a visit from a rich Mexican named Aaron Alonzo and his girlfriend, who had impressive credentials of her own. She was introduced as the niece of Senator Charles Percy. They promised him extra loan money.

When Abscam broke, Stanzyck discovered that his visitors

had actually been Aaron Sanchez and Kim Newboldt, who were both FBI agents. Stanzyck told Mike Wallace he believed that the FBI had been worried that if he had been too curious about Joe Meltzer, he could have blown the then-ongoing Abscam operation; hence the charade to try to convince him to pipe down.

::

In April 1981, William Webster, then the FBI director, testified before a congressional oversight committee about the Bureau's alleged complicity in the Meltzer affair. In his testimony, Webster asserted that the FBI "did not let people go down the drain in order to protect Meltzer or in order to protect Abscam."

He did say there might be other types of situations in the future and that there had been terrorism-related cases in the past. What Webster called "that hard philosophical issue" had come up before, citing the allegation that Winston Churchill had decided to let the British city of Coventry be bombed by the Luftwaffe in 1940 rather than show the Germans that the British had broken their Enigma code by protecting the targeted city. Such was not the case here, he said.

::

However, the same congressional committee heard from a number of people with their own horror stories about what had happened once they got involved with Joe Meltzer. Some had overextended themselves in anticipation of the loans. They had lost their businesses and were now bankrupt and unemployed. For others, banks had foreclosed on their homes. One person

---

WEBSTER'S FBI REIGN

William H. Webster became FBI director in February 1978 after serving as a United States Appeals Court Judge. Webster made white-collar crime a priority for the Bureau, and while he was director, a number of public corruption investigations were enacted, although the methods used were often controversial. The FBI got convictions against members of Congress with Abscam, the judiciary with an operation called Greylord, and members of state legislatures in California and South Carolina.

Greylord looked at corruption in the Cook County Circuit Court in Chicago. Almost one hundred people, including numerous judges and attorneys, were indicted and convicted as a result. Webster was FBI director until 1987. Another investigation begun under his watch, Operation Illwind, later turned up corruption in defense procurement. The most senior official convicted was Melvin Paisley, assistant secretary of the navy.

In 2001, Webster chaired the commission set up to investigate the espionage of FBI Special Agent Robert Hanssen.

---

had been sued by her landlord and had ended up on welfare. It had gotten so bad for Kai Gulve that he had tried to take his own life.

Kai Gulve: "I became so despondent, you know, and one night I just fired a gun, and—[*Laughs*]—at myself. And I don't know, I guess it wasn't my turn, 'cause it didn't fire. And

I got so mad, I—I pulled it out of my mouth and aimed it at the ceiling, and it naturally took off."

In San Diego, Mike Wallace talked to a roomful of people Joe Meltzer had conned. Almost all of them believed that Meltzer had been aided and abetted by the FBI. Mike Wallace heard the stories of people who'd contacted the FBI about Meltzer. One man said he'd talked with special agents in New York and Washington, D.C., both of whom had told him they knew Joe Meltzer, that he was working with them, and that he was an upstanding citizen.

Another man said he had been asked how he could have been so naive to have been taken in. He said that none of Meltzer's victims had been sophisticated enough to think they'd be ripped off with the knowledge and consent of the FBI.

::

In an endcap to the piece, Ed Bradley reiterated that no one at the FBI wanted to talk about Joe Meltzer, citing lawsuits that several of his victims had filed against the Bureau. The question remained, How much had the FBI known?

When he was arrested, Joe Meltzer signed a statement absolving the FBI of any knowledge of his scam. But later he said he had been coerced into signing that statement. Ed Bradley reported that House and Senate committees looking into the affair said they had found evidence that the FBI had known what Meltzer was up to and made a decision not to stop him for fear of exposing Abscam.

Wheeler, Dealer, Squealer

:: March 6, 1988 ::

Through the ages, law enforcement agencies have turned criminals into informers. This practice has always been fraught with ethical and practical dilemmas, and *60 Minutes* looked at three good examples. For one, should the FBI be paying people such as Mel Weinberg? The Meltzer case demonstrated what can happen when someone commits crimes under the cover of the protection afforded by the authorities. Still another problem might be that the crimes the individual was working off by helping the authorities had actually been worse than the ones he was helping to solve. How long can someone get away with serious offenses in exchange for information?

A few years after talking to Joe Meltzer, Mike Wallace met with Mike Raymond, who, like Meltzer, was a professional con man. Raymond had a much longer history with the FBI than did Meltzer. According to a top Justice Department official, Raymond was the Bureau's best informer. His deals had kept him largely out of jail over a thirty-year career that had included not only the swindling of millions of dollars from banks, brokerage houses, and individuals but more grievous crimes as well.

Raymond learned early on that by helping put away other criminals, he could avoid doing time himself. According to Raymond, echoing Mel Weinberg, the FBI will always need a crook to catch a crook because a con man is uniquely qualified to understand what's going on.

Mike Wallace: "Can the FBI do the job without you or somebody like you?"

Mike Raymond: "Not [on] the best day they ever lived. If you want to reduce it to an absolute quotient—"

Wallace: "Yeah."

Raymond: "It's a business relationship."

Mike Raymond was a somewhat heavyset man in his fifties with a large bald head. His glasses gave him an air of intelligence. Raymond did not look like a dangerous career criminal. Mike Raymond, or Mike Burnett, as he was also known, had an extensive resume of white-collar crimes: stealing securities, manipulating stocks, flimflamming banks. Raymond had at least twenty convictions that could have kept him in jail for the rest of his life had it not been for his repeated, not to say eager, readiness to cooperate with law enforcement.

Mike Wallace spoke about the use of informants with Stephen Trott, who supervised the Criminal Division of the Department of Justice. Trott said that almost any criminal could be used, as long as his evidence would hold up in court. He mentioned the "King of Heroin," Leroy "Nicky" Barnes, who'd testified against other heroin dealers in New York. The rule of thumb was not to use somebody unless it was absolutely necessary to pursue a very important objective.

In July 1984, Mike Raymond was arrested in Nashville as he was about to burglarize the home of a wealthy insurance executive. He was carrying a loaded machine gun with a silencer. The moment he was put in handcuffs, facing a twenty-year term if he was convicted, he started to cut a deal. It worked. Even as Raymond was being searched, he was told, "Don't worry about anything. Everything will work out all right."

Raymond's end of the bargain was to tell the FBI what his real job was. He was working for an outfit called Systematic Recovery Services, a collection agency that went after people who hadn't paid fines for traffic violations. Contracts for this service were worth a lot of money—the city of Chicago alone had $700 million in such outstanding fines. Raymond's job with Systematic Recovery Services was to make payoffs to politicians to secure the contracts to collect the fines. His deal with the FBI was to get the politicians to take the money in meetings that could be videotaped by the Bureau.

In Chicago, this undercover operation resulted in corruption charges being brought against twenty public officials, including Clarence McClain, who had dispensed patronage for the mayor, Harold Washington. Raymond first contacted McClain from a jail cell in Nashville, and the conversation was taped. McClain had been indicted and was awaiting trial when Mike Wallace spoke with him. According to McClain, Raymond was the one who should have been facing the music, not him.

Clarence McClain: "What Mike Raymond done with the help of some overenthusiastic federal employees—"

Mike Wallace: "Federal employees."

McClain: "—is attempt to entrap me, lie, cheat, and steal. To do anything they could rather than be incarcerated. They have not succeeded."

INFORMANT-AT-LARGE

Leroy "Nicky" Barnes was the head of an enormous heroin-selling operation in New York City in the 1970s. The DEA said more than 2,100 people died of drug overdoses in the city between 1973 and 1979, and that most were caused by heroin supplied by Barnes's organization. Barnes was frequently arrested, but no charge ever stuck, leading to his being pictured on the cover of *The New York Times Magazine* under the title "Mr. Untouchable."

That irked then-President Jimmy Carter, and through the attorney general and the U.S. attorney in New York, Barnes was indicted, convicted, and sentenced to life without parole.

Nicky Barnes told his story to Mike Wallace in 1986. His career as an FBI informant began after he was sent to prison. Barnes found out that the two women in his life had started intimate relationships with former business partners of his, and he contacted the feds. Using the drug kingpin's testimony, the government got convictions against many members of Barnes's former inner circle.

McClain claimed that Raymond made it sound as if he had been accepting a bribe. All he had really been doing, he said, was talking about the reimbursement of some expenses Raymond owed him. According to McClain, Raymond had asked him how he wanted the money—twenties, fifties, or hundreds? McClain had said he didn't care how he got the money, he just wanted his expenses paid. Phil Parenti, McClain's attorney, asserted that Raymond had manufactured the crime, that there had been nothing illegal or clandestine about the money transfer.

While Barnes may have started informing out of a desire for revenge, he went on cooperating in the hopes of getting a presidential pardon. He testified before a commission on organized crime and even against fellow prison inmates.

Despite Barnes's lurid history—he virtually admitted to Mike Wallace that he had had people killed—some people in the Justice Department thought Barnes's cooperation had earned him his freedom. Among his supporters was a U.S. attorney for the southern district of New York, Rudolph Giuliani. Giuliani said that rewarding informers was "the only way we can combat this kind of activity."

In 1986 Mike Wallace reported that Justice officials said that the best Nicky Barnes could hope for was a reduction in his life sentence and parole sometime in the next ten years. In August 1998, it was reported that Nicky Barnes had been released from prison after serving twenty-one years, given a new identity, and been admitted into the Witness Protection [relocation] Program.

Mike Raymond remembered the relationship differently. When he had met with Clarence McClain, he said, McClain had made no bones about the fact that he was Mayor Washington's confidant and that he could deliver whatever Raymond wanted in Chicago. Furthermore, McClain had said that he was "the only man that could put money in Harold Washington's hand."

Mayor Washington died in office in 1987. He was never charged with accepting a bribe from Mike Raymond. Former Chicago alderman Clifford Kelley was one of the city officials who was charged, and he pleaded guilty to mail fraud and federal income tax violations, offenses for which he was given a one-year sentence. Kelley told Mike Wallace that Raymond had practically insisted he take money from him. He admitted that Raymond had been extremely successful in convincing his victims he was who he said he was.

But Mike Raymond's work for the FBI in Chicago was nothing more than a con game, albeit one played for the benefit of the authorities. He ran his operation from his living room on the fifteenth floor of Lakepoint Towers in Chicago. He invited some of the city's most prominent politicians to his apartment, and the FBI videotaped the proceedings from the neighboring apartment. He would make lunch or dinner for his guests. There'd be food and a little wine, a convivial setting for a conversation.

Clifford Kelley: "He begged me to come for dinner. One of the other gentlemen who went to dinner with him was, you know, he said, 'What is with this guy?' You know, 'Doesn't he have any friends? Why has he got to have dinner with us?' We—"

Mike Wallace: "He begged you because he wanted you on
      tape."
Kelley: "Absolutely. And he had every reason to want us on
      tape."

While Mike Raymond was busy working undercover, helping the
FBI catch politicians in Chicago, there was reason to believe he
might be involved in a number of other cases across the country.
These weren't money crimes or the kind of scheme Raymond was
helping to unravel in Chicago. According to internal documents,
the FBI used Raymond despite the fact that it was aware that he
was a suspect in three possible murders.

One of the murder victims was a Fort Lauderdale woman
named Adelaide Stiles, who had been killed in the mid-1970s.
The lead investigator into Stiles's death was Captain Al Ortenzo.
Ortenzo said he had tried to get the FBI to help with the case but
had run up against a stone wall. He had asked the FBI permission
to interview Raymond about it, but he was denied access. It was an
experience he described as "one of the most frustrating" he'd had
in dealing with any law enforcement or criminal justice agency.

In 1985, the Fort Lauderdale police broke the Stiles case and
charged Mike Raymond with the crime. They were able to do so
thanks to the testimony of yet another con man, a colleague of
Raymond's named Vernon Frazier, who did to Raymond what
Raymond had done to numerous others over the years: he turned
him in to avoid going to jail himself.

Vernon Frazier told the police that Raymond had romanced
Stiles before stealing her money. When the widow had asked for
her money back, Raymond had taken her out on a boat and had

her killed. Frazier told Mike Wallace what had happened on the boat ride. He said Stiles and Raymond had been downstairs on the boat, laughing and talking. Raymond was saying how much he loved her and that he'd never do anything to hurt her. Stiles told Raymond she loved him back and trusted him. That was when Frazier hit her with a tire iron. As he recalled, the last thing she said sounded like "Why?"

According to Frazier, Adelaide Stiles's body had been chopped up and thrown overboard under the supervision of Mike Raymond. Frazier said that Raymond had been present at the murder and that he'd testify to that at Raymond's trial. Raymond's version was that he had neither murdered Adelaide Stiles nor caused her to be murdered. Every allegation against him, everything that Vernon Frazier accused him of, was false. According to William Aronwald, his attorney, Raymond had had a business relationship with her, simple as that.

Mike Wallace spoke with Fort Lauderdale police captain Al Ortenzo.

Mike Wallace: "What would you like to see happen to Michael Raymond?"

Captain Ortenzo: "I'd like to see Michael Raymond get a fair trial and go directly to the electric chair without passing go, collecting two hundred dollars or any more pay and benefits from the FBI."

Mike Wallace laid out a scenario for Vernon Frazier. His testimony, if found believable by the jury, would put Raymond away for a long, long time. And there were people in the Fort Lauderdale police department who wanted to see him go to the electric chair. Frazier said he understood that. Was that all right with him? Yes, it was, he said.

Raymond said he didn't need to kill anyone to take $40,000 from her. As for Vernon Frazier, Raymond said he hadn't met him until 1984, nine years after Adelaide Stiles had disappeared. Raymond said he'd used Frazier only for his Chicago sting operation, in which Frazier's function had been to act as a black connection to get to Clarence McClain. Chicago had nothing to do with what Raymond described as the Stiles "nonsense."

Vernon Frazier told Mike Wallace that the State of Florida had offered to charge him with anything from second-degree murder down to zero in the Stiles case if he would testify for it. As Mike Wallace said, it wasn't as though Frazier would just turn himself in, say "I did it," and go to the electric chair. There was a quid pro quo, which was to turn in Mike Raymond.

::

But in August 1987, Raymond's attorney began turning up inconsistencies in Frazier's story. Among them was the fact that on the night of the murder, the boat that was used for the crime would have had to pass under a low bridge, an impossibility, according to William Aronwald, because the boat rode too high in the water. Aronwald said he believed that Frazier had gotten the details of the crime from the Fort Lauderdale police and was simply parroting them back. He was its only witness, and if his story were deemed credible, Mike Raymond would be found guilty.

Mike Wallace: "Hell of a spot to be in, age of fifty-eight, conned, stolen, swindled, but at work for the FBI, and your life's in danger."

Mike Raymond: "Yes, a very unhappy situation."

Vernon Frazier told Mike Wallace what he had learned from Raymond about conning people. He told him that he'd be satisfied if he knew 5 or 10 percent of what Raymond knew. Wallace wanted to know how he could be sure Frazier wasn't pulling a con on him right there. Frazier said he had nothing to gain by conning Wallace. There was nothing Wallace could give him or do for him.

Mike Wallace: "In court it's going to be the word of one con man, you, against another con man—and a better con man than you."

Vernon Frazier: "Correct. And as I said, may the best con win."

Two days after that interview, before Vernon Frazier ever got to testify in court, he recanted his entire confession to his part in Adelaide Stiles's murder. Raymond's attorney had proved that he was a liar. Frazier later said he had been coerced into making his statement and fabricating the story by a Fort Lauderdale detective who had promised him, in addition to a light sentence, a possible role in a movie about the case. When Frazier did meet Mike Raymond in court, it was to watch the judge dismiss all the charges.

That wasn't the end of Mike Raymond's story. He was picked up by the feds again and held on parole violation. He immediately began talking to his attorney about a possible deal. Raymond's attorney may have forgotten he was wearing a *60 Minutes* microphone when his client started talking about a plan forming in his mind . . .

Mike Raymond: "That's the understatement of the century."
William Aronwald: "Okay, so fine, so I have to talk to—"
Raymond: "I'm sitting on dynamite. It's gonna explode."
Aronwald: "Mike—"
Raymond: "Bill, the first haul, that was three and a half million in cash. I wish—I want twenty percent."

In 1996, the *Chicago Tribune* reported that Michael Raymond, aka Michael Burnett, had died in his cell at the U.S. Penitentiary in Atlanta at the age of sixty-seven. Raymond had suffered from heart disease and other ailments, and there were no indications of foul play. In March 1995, in a Brooklyn federal district court, Raymond had been convicted of directing the murder of his accomplice in a counterfeit check scheme he had run at a Staten Island bank in the early 1990s.

Raymond

The Secret Life of Dennis Levine

:: September 22, 1991 ::

Dennis Levine was involved in one of the biggest scandals ever to hit Wall Street, a massive insider trading ring that was exposed in 1986. Some of the biggest names in the financial world were taken down: Michael Milken, Ivan Boesky, and Martin Siegel. Levine spent time in Lewisburg penitentiary for illegally sharing inside information and trading on it. When he got out, he wrote a book about his experiences. Ed Bradley met Levine in 1991. He was much more interested in what Levine had been up to after he was released from jail than what had gotten him into trouble in the first place.

Bradley began by returning to the heady days of the 1980s. Levine was a trader at the rising firm of Drexel Burnham Lambert. He would often work his insider deals using a private line in his office. When that phone rang, Levine told Ed Bradley, it was "like

Dennis Levine

a cash register going off." Levine recalled a particularly successful day he had trading inside information on Nabisco stock in 1985:

Dennis Levine: "No sooner did the stock open than my phone lit up like a Christmas tree and each of the people involved called to say, 'How'd we do?' It was this incredible feeling of invulnerability, of a rush, that in pushing a button, in making two phone calls, I made close to three million dollars. And that's what drove it. That was the insanity of it all. It wasn't that hard."

So easy was it that in five years Levine managed to hide $12.6 million in a secret Bahamian bank account. But that wasn't enough. Levine told Ed Bradley that as he had gotten bolder and bolder, it had become easier—and he'd made more and more money. Looking back, he said, he realized he had been sick. It had been an addiction. He had been living for the high of making the next deal, the bigger deal. He had never thought he would be caught.

But on May 12, 1986, Dennis Levine was caught. He was accused of making $12.6 million from insider trading. Levine later pled guilty to charges of securities fraud, tax evasion, and perjury. He cooperated with the authorities, turning in members of his own ring and the arbitrageur Ivan Boesky. He did fifteen months in Lewisburg Federal Penitentiary in Pennsylvania and was released in 1988. When Ed Bradley spoke with him, Levine said he had turned his life around. He was running a financial consulting firm and lecturing students around the country on the lessons he said he'd learned from his own mistakes.

In his lectures, Dennis Levine sounded like the epitome of the contrite ex-con trying to make his way back in the world. He was filmed delivering a homily from the podium. Levine told his audience that he adhered to a "higher standard." Before we do something, he said, we should step back and ask if it was something we'd like to read about on the front page of *The Wall Street Journal* tomorrow. If the answer is "yes," we're probably doing something right. If not, we shouldn't do it.

Ed Bradley: "Do you think that you would ever do anything clearly illegal again?"

Dennis Levine: "Not only wouldn't I do something clearly illegal, I wouldn't even get close. Once burned, Ed, you don't go near the fire. I've learned a lesson."

Bradley: "What about something that's unethical? Would you draw the line there?"

Levine: "Yes."

That assertion, offered with apparent sincerity, would have surprised two men who had done business with Dennis Levine since his release from jail. Randy Jochim and Tom Brechtel were businessmen who hired Levine as their financial adviser about eighteen months after he got out of Lewisburg.

Jochim and Brechtel were not especially big players by the standards of Wall Street circa 1985, but the two men had what must have looked like an excellent business opportunity to them. They wanted to develop an oceanfront property at Laguna Niguel in California. Levine was taken on to help them find financing to build luxury homes on a plot of land that looked down on a majestic swath of Pacific beach. Levine was paid upfront fees of $10,000, but all of them expected to share in a profit of $14 million.

One of Levine's responsibilities was to run due diligence checks on the people and companies he recommended. He was to check out their legitimacy and make sure they had the financial wherewithal to do a given deal. Levine took Jochim and Brechtel to Panama and introduced them to two companies, Morgan Gundy and Pan-Global. Pan-Global said it would lend $32 million as long as Jochim and Brechtel paid up-front fees of about $150,000. After Levine told the two men it was a good deal, they handed to Pan-Global the up-front money.

Dennis Levine sold the Pan-Global deal hard to Jochim and Brechtel. He was a miracle worker. He danced and jumped up and down and told the men how great this was, how their lives had changed. "It sent goosebumps up and down my spine," said Jochim. "It felt good, you know. It felt great."

Ed Bradley asked Dennis Levine what had made him think that these companies were substantial entities that had this kind of funding to invest. Levine said that a client of his had stated "unequivocally" that someone else had received funding from them. But he admitted he had carried out no investigation beyond that recommendation. Ed Bradley asked Dennis Levine if he had been aware that neither Pan-Global nor Morgan Gundy had ever done deals in Panama like this with anyone. Levine said he had had information that they had done deals in the past. Ed Bradley wondered if he had known that the two companies were being investigated by the FBI. Levine replied that he had had no specific knowledge of that.

It turned out that many companies had paid up-front fees to Pan-Global in a similar fashion as Jochim and Brechtel, and none had received any money back. The U.S. Embassy in Panama and the Commerce Department both warned businesses to stay away from them.

::

Jochim and Brechtel's Pan-Global deal fell through, but Levine was able to convince the two men that he had found another lender, this time in Florida. Business was getting more expensive. This time it would cost them $25,000 for the introduction from Levine and a further $300,000 up front to secure the $23 million in financing. Short the $150,000 they had left in Panama, the developers didn't have that kind of money. But Levine found a man called Bob Amira, a businessman from Las Vegas. Levine said Amira could find them a venture partner who would put up the up-front money in exchange for some of the back-end profits.

Tom Brechtel said that Levine had characterized Amira as an associate, someone he had known during his days at Drexel. Ed Bradley asked Levine if he'd checked Amira out before recommending him. He said he hadn't.

Ed Bradley: "But isn't that part of what you do—check out companies, check out individuals?"

Dennis Levine: "All I did was make an introduction."

Bradley: "Were you aware that he's a convicted thief—"

Levine: "No."

Bradley: "—that he has ties to the New York Mafia?"

Levine: "I had no idea."

Amira had in fact been convicted of theft for his part in a credit scheme that had netted more than $700,000 from two Atlantic City casinos. It was a scheme that state investigators characterized as having been engineered by the New York mob. Levine said that he had been approached by Amira, who'd said that he could get loans and do real estate transactions. Levine had thought that Amira had expertise and contacts that he lacked himself.

When the Amira connection didn't work for Jochim and Brechtel, Levine came up with yet another possibility, a man named Jim Massaro. Massaro was supposed to help get access to the money available in Florida. Tom Brechtel thought that Massaro was another one of Levine's Drexel contacts. When Ed Bradley asked Levine how he had known Jim Massaro, Levine said he'd known him from the time he'd spent in Lewisburg. They'd spent almost nine months together in the jail.

Ed Bradley asked Levine if he'd told Jochim and Brechtel

how he'd met Massaro. He said he wasn't sure they'd known. Neither could he recall having told them that Massaro had been convicted of business fraud. Why didn't Dennis Levine tell his clients about the background of the individuals he was recommending they work with? Levine asked, "Why?" He said that would have made him a hypocrite. Levine's clients had known what his background was. He hadn't hidden it and had been very up front about it. When pressed, Levine said that perhaps he should have told them. Why hadn't he? All he'd wanted to do, he said, was help Tom and Randy.

Jochim and Brechtel finally did meet the Florida-based investor, a company called Earnscliffe Trust, headed by Robert Wilson, who was represented as what Brechtel called "a big wheel in the lending business at the high level." A photograph showed Wilson at a business function in American Samoa. The camera moved up this large man's body: loafers, what looked like a wrap skirt, and a garland of flowers decorating a plain T-shirt. Another man involved, Lee Lybarger was, as far as Brechtel knew, a "heavy hitter." Throughout this period, Brechtel and Jochim were relying on Dennis Levine's judgment. If Levine brought them someone, he was okay.

Levine told Jochim and Brechtel that his latest contacts were part of a new operation that had developed a novel concept and was expanding. He said they had good references that had checked out. When Ed Bradley asked Levine who'd checked them out, he said that clients had, and he himself had. But he was unaware of the fact that Lybarger was a convicted thief. "I didn't do a background check on that, no."

A check on Lybarger turned up a mug shot of a man wearing the kind of wide tie that was a trademark of the 1970s, along with oversize glasses and a good deal of hair parted on the side and swept over the crown. Lybarger had defrauded at least four people of more than $120,000 in a scam in the early 1980s, and in December 1990, he had been arrested on charges of running an up-front-fees scam in New Orleans. Levine was also unaware of anything untoward about Robert Wilson—not the outstanding legal judgments against him or the unfulfilled promises to other businessmen.

In fact, Earnscliffe had taken in at least $2.5 million in advance fees and never paid out a dime in return. It had no assets, its banking and credit references were phony, and it wasn't licensed to operate in Florida—nor anywhere in the United States, for that matter, in any capacity as a financial services firm. That's what *60 Minutes's* background check showed. Bradley wondered if Levine's background check had showed something different.

Levine had already asserted that Earnscliffe had checked out. It had lawyers; it had people representing them; it had bank references. When he had discussed the firm with clients, he had told them Earnscliffe was new, it had just opened an office. Levine said he'd never told anyone anything that wasn't true. In March 1991, the Florida comptroller's office shut down Earnscliffe Trust, alleging that it had bilked customers out of up-front fees for loans that had never been made. Brechtel and Jochim had struck out again. They didn't get any money from Wilson, either.

Ed Bradley sounded as though he were getting increasingly exasperated with Levine.

Ed Bradley: "What does all of this look like?"

Dennis Levine: "What?"

Bradley: "You know, I—I hate to say it, Dennis, but it just doesn't, on the surface, look good."

Levine: "Then let's look beyond the surface. Let's get right down to the specifics and the documents."

Bradley: "But each time I get down to the specifics of the people involved, I don't see due diligence on your part. I'm trying to give you the benefit of the doubt—"

Levine: "Right."

Bradley: "—to tell me how you came up with these people, who are a group of convicted con men, thieves."

Levine insisted that the story as Bradley was telling it was unbalanced. Insisting on the rectitude of his own information, Dennis Levine handed over more than eight hundred pages of documents that would, he claimed, provide a totally different version.

The documents provided, brandished by Ed Bradley in two big binders, did nothing to exonerate Dennis Levine. There was no evidence that he had performed the due diligence he claimed on the people and companies he had introduced to Jochim and Brechtel. Nor was there anything to prove that Pan-Global or Earnscliffe Trust had ever funded a deal.

On one document, Levine had clumsily covered with Wite-Out the name of a company he'd advised. The Wite-Out was scratched off to reveal the number, and *60 Minutes* called it. The president of the company concerned said that he too had been introduced to Pan-Global and Earnscliffe and had paid fees to

Levine. But he had had suspicions about the companies and pulled out after paying Levine $20,000. Randy Jochim and Tom Brechtel said they were out more than $200,000.

Ed Bradley: "What would you say to people who would accuse you of being a con man?"

Dennis Levine: "That's absolutely false. I have never conned anybody in my life, nor would I."

Bradley: "I mean, some people have described you as a consummate con man, that—even to the point that sometimes you con yourself. What would you say to that?"

Levine: "People are entitled to their own opinions, but it's not true. I have to live with myself. I don't think I've done anything wrong."

When the piece was rebroadcast a year later, Lesley Stahl reported that a federal grand jury had been convened to look into Dennis Levine's latest business dealings and that Tom Brechtel and Randy Jochim had filed a $20 million lawsuit against him.

The full story of the huge financial scandal that landed Levine in trouble in the first place is told in James B. Stewart's best-seller *Den of Thieves*. Levine features prominently in the book.

In an update for the paperback edition, Stewart wrote about Levine's appearance on *60 Minutes*. Levine had come to the interview thinking he was going to talk about *Inside Out,* the book he had written about his experiences and his new life after jail. Instead, he was confronted with Ed Bradley's questions about Brechtel and Jochim's aborted business venture.

Levine's confident demeanor waned visibly as the interview pro-
gressed.

Levine was hit with more civil suits after the program aired,
and his book tour was canceled. James Stewart wrote that he had
been highly visible in Manhattan, living on Park Avenue and eating at the Four Seasons, one of New York's most prominent
power lunch spots. After his unexpected grilling on national television, he adopted a significantly lower profile.

A Family Affair

:: April 11, 1999 ::

After Sante Kimes and her son, Kenneth, were arrested in New York in the summer of 1998, they were frequently referred to in the media as "grifters." The Kimeses were linked with a litany of crimes across the country—from shoplifting and credit card fraud to arson and murder. The term "grifter" seemed almost quaint in the light of some of the allegations against them. If the unusual mother-and-son team did make some people think of the characters in Jim Thompson's novel *The Grifters* and the subsequent movie, their criminal activities went far beyond the con games usually associated with grift.

Most seriously, authorities in a number of jurisdictions were anxious to talk to the Kimeses about people who had disappeared after having dealings with them. In the Bahamas, they were wanted for questioning about the disappearance of a banker. They were also suspects in the murder of a businessman in Los Angeles. In New York they were accused of killing an elderly woman and getting rid of the body. But in each of these cases there was very little other than circumstantial evidence against them.

Sante and Kenneth Kimes

Before their trial for murder in New York and while they were being held without bail, the Kimeses appeared on television, something that suspects in a murder case very rarely do. The Kimeses hadn't even been photographed together before they went on national television. Kenneth Kimes said they wanted to speak out because of what he described as the unfair portrayal of them in the media. They were, Mrs. Kimes said, "just a mother and son."

The Kimeses' chosen forum was *60 Minutes*. Steve Kroft spoke with them at Manhattan Detention Center. As he sat down with the two of them, he said that setting up the interview had been like arranging the Paris Peace Talks. He gestured toward a gaggle of lawyers who were sitting overseeing the interview. Kroft had been warned by the Kimeses' legal team that because of the investigations and legal proceedings, there were many questions their clients couldn't, or shouldn't, answer.

The Kimeses were charged with murdering eighty-two-year-old Irene Silverman of Manhattan. The indictment said that Kenneth Kimes had moved into an apartment in Silverman's $7 million building using a false name. It was alleged that the Kimeses had then tried to get the widow to sign the building over to them using a variety of subterfuges. When they failed to persuade Mrs. Silverman to do what they wanted, prosecutors said, they killed her. There was, however, no physical evidence that Mrs. Silverman had been harmed, let alone murdered. In fact, her body was never found.

Sante Kimes said there was no truth to the charges. Steve Kroft mentioned some of the things the Kimeses had been called: "the queen and prince of con artists, Bonnie and son of Clyde, mother and son grifters," and, by the New York district attorney, "cold-blooded killers." As his mother shook her head incredulously, Kenneth Kimes said the DA was an unfair source. Mrs. Kimes said the DA had no evidence.

Steve Kroft: "You don't like the term 'grifters.'"
Sante Kimes: "Well, the reason I don't like the term 'grifters,' Mr. Kroft, is that we—we—"
Kenneth Kimes: "It's so derogatory."
Sante Kimes: "—we lived—we lived in one ho—we've lived where we've lived. We're not drifters or grifters, or—I don't even know where the word came from."

THE GRIFTER

In David Maurer's classic 1940 study of the confidence man, *The Big Con,* a grifter is "in the strict sense, one who lives by his wits as contrasted to the heavy-men who use violence," although "grift" in the wider sense meant a racket or the criminal profession.

Maurer's book, which served as the basis of the movie *The Sting,* is a treasure trove of confidence games of all kinds and their extraordinary practitioners. "Confidence men trade upon certain weaknesses in human nature," Maurer wrote. "Hence until human nature changes perceptibly there is little possibility that there will be a shortage of marks for con games."

::

Sante Kimes fixed on the notion that real grifters would be nomadic, following their crimes around. Far from drifting, Sante Kimes said, her family had lived for long periods in both Nevada and Hawaii. The Kimes family had indeed lived in Las Vegas and Honolulu. Both of their residences had met a similar fate: one home had been destroyed in a fire, the other severely damaged by one. Investigators said the fires might have been set to try to collect insurance money. Steve Kroft wanted to address the reason for the grifters comment by talking about Sante Kimes's criminal record, but he was cut off by one of the lawyers.

The lawyers were anxious to keep Mrs. Kimes's forty-year-long arrest record out of court. The charges against her were mostly for larceny, nothing approaching murder, and there were only a couple of convictions. In 1980, for example, Sante Kimes was caught taking a mink coat from the Mayflower Hotel in Washington. That particular case made it to trial, but she left town while the jury was out. That had all been a misunderstanding, she said, one of many that had left her with a bad reputation.

The details of the alleged crimes somehow didn't seem to fit the couple as they appeared before the cameras. The Kimeses were interviewed in a room holding what looked like leather-bound legal casebooks. Mrs. Kimes wore a light blue pantsuit and had put her hair up. With her reading glasses on, she could pass for a schoolteacher. Her son's dark suit and conservative blue tie spoke of a young professional man.

::

The real story of the family was nothing so conventional. The late Kenneth Kimes, Sr., had been a millionaire builder and motel owner. In 1974, the couple had their photograph taken with Gerald and Betty Ford, although apparently they had crashed the White House function where the picture came from. Sante Kimes said her husband had been a wonderful man, a big old Irishman. Her son looked a lot like him. Kenneth said his mom was "a very wonderful, beautiful mom. I think she's a beautiful person, spiritually and intellectually and—and physically." That made Sante Kimes laugh.

Kenneth Kimes said that kindness was a key consideration in his own friendships and relationships. "Do unto others as you would have done unto yourself." As Steve Kroft said, this admirable sentiment did not seem to apply to his mother when it came to the women she employed as maids. In the 1980s, Sante Kimes was convicted of slavery, of holding domestic workers at her homes in Nevada and Hawaii against their will. She was accused of burning one with an iron. She spent three years in federal prison even though she denied abusing the maids and maintained that the women had just been out to get her husband's money.

Gerald and Betty Ford with Sante
Kimes and her late husband

Mrs. Kimes was asked whether she and her son were honest people. She said Kenny was especially, and "I think I am." In business, she said, you have to be sharp. Kenneth Kimes, Sr., had taught her that there are a lot of people who will try to cheat you. Her husband had worried that she didn't have a good head for business because she was an extravagant spender. Kenneth Kimes said with a laugh that his mother was good at shopping, and she agreed: she was good at spending money, not making it.

::

It was difficult to find out just who Sante Kimes was. Authorities said she'd used more than twenty aliases, names such as Sandra Chambers, Donna Lawson, and Joy Landis. Off camera, Sante Kimes said she had used the aliases to hide from Panamanian drug dealers she'd informed against and who were trying to kill her.

To try to find out more, Steve Kroft asked the Kimeses' four-strong legal team some extremely basic factual questions. Such as when and where she had been born. One asked what that had to do with whether or not a case could be proven against them. Steve Kroft said she had two birth dates on record. Les Levine, Mrs. Kimes's investigator, stepped in.

Les Levine: "I can tell you that my own experience is that when we try to do a background on individuals, sometimes individuals come up with as many as a half a dozen Social Security numbers; doesn't make them criminals."

Steve Kroft: "Mrs. Kimes has two of those."

Levine: "Many people are linked to more than one Social Security number. And again, it doesn't make them a criminal."

Steve Kroft suggested to the Kimeses that they were in a pretty big mess. "Not by our choice," said Kenneth. When Steve Kroft asked how, then one of the lawyers stopped the interview again.

Perhaps they got into a mess because odd things happened to people who knew them—Elmer Holmgren, for instance. He came forward after the Kimeses' house in Hawaii burned down

Sante Kimes's mug shot

and told federal agents he'd done it for the Kimes family. Before a case could be brought, Holmgren told his family he was going to Central America with Mr. and Mrs. Kimes, and he was never heard from again. Les Levine said he had no idea what had happened to Elmer Holmgren. And no one was quite sure what happened to Syed Bilal Ahmed, a bank executive who had done business with Sante Kimes. He was believed to have been with her in the Bahamas on September 4, 1996. At least two bank employees said that Ahmed had told them he planned to have dinner with Mrs. Kimes that night to talk about bank business. He went back to his hotel and hasn't been seen since.

Mr. Ahmed's family hired a private investigator, Ken Hawkins. Of Sante Kimes, Hawkins said, "Wherever she turns up, people seem to disappear." Hawkins agreed that the evidence against Mrs. Kimes in the case he was dealing with was entirely circumstantial. Steve Kroft wondered whether it couldn't just be a coincidence: because Mrs. Kimes had a record as a "bunko artist," whenever someone disappeared, suspicion turned to her. It could be a coinci-

THE POET AND THE PEASANT

Steve Kroft mentioned the term "bunko artist." A "bunco" or "bunko" is a swindle, and in the nineteenth century, a "bunko steerer" was someone who led a mark to his fate, usually in a card game. ("Bunkum" is associated more with insincerity than criminality, coming from "Buncombe," the district represented by Felix Walker in the sixteenth Congress. Walker said that a particularly irrelevant speech he was making was for his constituents rather than the whole house.)

In O. Henry's short story "The Poet and the Peasant," an innocent country-dweller arrives in New York City dressed in such a stereotypically rustic outfit, topped with a wisp of hay in his hair, that the seen-it-all New Yorkers he encounters assume he must be in costume for some kind of con game.

At Eighth Avenue stands "Bunco Harry," who personifies the knowing metropolitan professional. "Harry was too good an artist not to be pained at the sight of an actor overdoing his part," the story goes. "He edged up to the countryman, who had stopped to open his mouth at a jewelry store window, and shook his head. 'Too thick, pal,' he said, critically. 'Too thick by a couple of inches.'"

dence, said Ken Hawkins. But if so, it was a case of "coincidence upon coincidence upon coincidence." If you put it together with what he knew and with what people in law enforcement had said, it would seem to be more than a coincidence.

::

In one of the cases that prosecutors were trying to link with the Kimeses, there *was* a body. In March 1998, David Kazdin, an old acquaintance of the Kimes family, was found shot to death in a Dumpster near Los Angeles airport. Kazdin's attorney, Phil Eaton, said he told police he thought he could tell them who their number one suspect should be.

Eaton said Kazdin had told him he'd allowed the Kimeses to put his name on a deed to their home in Las Vegas as a favor. Someone had then taken out a fraudulent $280,000 mortgage after forging his signature. Kazdin told Eaton he felt that Sante Kimes was behind it. She'd left him messages saying they needed to talk. The last time the two men had spoken, Kazdin had said, "This woman's crazy—she'll do anything." Eaton didn't feel that Kazdin had been panicked, but Kazdin was concerned. A week later Kazdin's body was found in a Dumpster.

L.A. prosecutors said they had probable cause to arrest the Kimeses for David Kazdin's murder, but at the time of the broadcast no charges had been filed. The Kimeses' lawyer Mel Sachs asked for the proof against the pair in the disappearances. There had been too much speculation, he said. The only place they had been charged was in New York in connection with the disappearance of Irene Silverman.

Sante Kimes: "We don't know where this woman is. Wherever she is, I pray to God she's all right."

Off camera, Sante Kimes told Steve Kroft she had liked Irene Silverman. They used to drink champagne together. Kimes said Silverman had told her she wanted to travel abroad, maybe to

Europe. But prosecutors said that would have been difficult, because the Kimeses were in possession of Silverman's passport when they were arrested. The police had a list of items found in the Kimeses' possession which also included, along with Silverman's keys, a forged deed to her house, a stun gun, handcuffs, hypodermic syringes, a knockout drug, and a loaded 9 mm pistol. The Kimeses' legal team had something to say about that.

Les Levine: "All—all of these issues, I'm sure, will be addressed at the time of trial. But you've mentioned half a dozen means of disposing of somebody. What are you supposed to do—multiple choice? How did Mrs. Silverman, if she is dead, how—did she meet her death? By hypodermic needle? By stun gun? You pick the one that you think fits the crime and convict them on that."

The Kimeses maintained that they had been framed by the police, unfairly treated by the judge, and convicted in the press. Kenneth Kimes, whose hand was clasped in his mother's throughout the interview, said that he'd heard rumors that he didn't love his mother and other "bizarre, bizarre" comments that were "so tabloid-based . . . so full of hate."

Kenneth Kimes said that before the arrest he had been just a normal guy. He had been on a dating show on MTV. "Hi, Candace, my name is Ken," he had said into the camera in the flirtatious tone people try to use in such a situation. "I want to be the big guy in your life." And he'd been doing all right at the University of California, Santa Barbara, when he'd left in 1996.

Steve Kroft wanted to ask about Kenneth Kimes's college

career. He said that he'd seen Kimes's college transcript. "I see you got an A in acting." With that, one of the Kimeses' legal team stopped the interview again. "Stop, stop, come on. That's not a fair question, acting," he said. That ended the interview for good. Mrs. Kimes said, "I'm no angel, but I'm no murderer either. . . . If you knew my real story, it would explain a lot."

::

In the spring of 2000, Sante and Kenneth Kimes were convicted of the murder of Irene Silverman in addition to a host of lesser related crimes—she, fifty-eight in all; he, sixty. Sante Kimes was sentenced to 120 years in jail and Kenneth, 125. They were subsequently extradited to California to face trial for the murder of David Kazdin. If convicted of that offense, the pair could face the death penalty.

Before he was sent to California, Kenneth Kimes took Maria Zone, a Court TV producer, hostage when she came to interview him in jail. He held her for four hours, using a ballpoint pen as a weapon. His principal demand was that his mother not be taken to California to face the murder charge.

Nick Leeson

In Over His Head

:: September 10, 1995 ::

Over the years, *60 Minutes* has investigated a number of brokers, dealers, traders, and bankers operating unlawfully on the far reaches of the speculative side of the financial business. Perhaps the most spectacular case involved Nicholas Leeson, a twenty-eight-year-old Englishman who single-handedly destroyed one of Britain's most prestigious financial institutions. He did so while trying to cover up losses he'd made in the markets. But he was adamant that of the hundreds of millions of dollars involved, he'd taken not so much as a single penny for himself.

In September 1995, Steve Kroft looked at the Leeson affair on the eve of an interview Leeson was giving the BBC, his first since being captured after several days on the run. Leeson was being held in a six-by-twelve-foot jail cell in a prison outside Frankfurt, Germany, while he fought extradition back to Singapore. Leeson had worked in Singapore as a securities trader for Barings Bank.

The venerable Barings was founded way back in 1763, when America was still a colony. It was old enough to have helped finance the Louisiana Purchase, and it was trusted sufficiently to handle the finances of Queen Elizabeth II. Leeson's job was trading derivatives; specifically, futures and options, which amounted to huge bets on the future direction of the Japanese stock market.

Nick Leeson

Steve Kroft noted that although you might wonder how one person could destroy a bank, in the era of high-speed computers and complicated investments, it doesn't take a genius to do it. And by conventional standards, Leeson was no genius. He'd never been to college, and it was widely reported that he had failed high school math. Even in Singapore, he was a junior employee in the Barings universe who just a few years before had been a clerk in London's financial district. But he was able to run amok unsupervised on the Singapore trading floor.

Part of Leeson's responsibility was to keep the books. He lost money in some trades, and rather than report what had happened, he found a place to hide it in the system he knew very well. He created a secret account numbered 88888. Leeson said he had called it that because eight is considered a lucky number by Chinese people. He claimed he had first used the account to hide honest mistakes from his superiors in London. His losses mounted, until by the end of 1992 they reached $3 million.

Leeson was digging a hole for himself. As the deficits piled up, he continued his deception and worked to be in a position where he could replace the funds when the market moved in the right direction. To Leeson, the increasingly huge sums involved didn't seem like real money. It's not as though he had the cash sitting there in front of him. When he was interviewed, the reckless trader turned out to be a fresh-faced young man with a quiet voice and a slight suburban London accent. He spoke to David Frost about his battle to recoup his losses.

Nick Leeson: "As crazy as it may seem, you know, there were days when I was—when I could lose twenty-five million, thirty million pounds. There were days when I made fifty million pounds based off the position. Not every day is a down day."

But Leeson had more than enough down days. In the first half of 1994, his losses went from $37 million to more than $150 million. Because Leeson was reporting only his gains, not his losses, he could go to the racetrack or the cricket club or the company yacht and act the star that everyone assumed him to be. He was having an apparently unbroken run of successes. Far from relishing the approbation, Leeson told the BBC he had hated every minute of the act as he worked desperately to keep up appearances.

Leeson's problems multiplied after the Kobe earthquake in Japan in January 1995, which hit the Japanese stock market hard and devastated the remnants of Leeson's investments. He began to be pressured to pay up by the exchanges in Japan and Singapore. He had to wire London repeatedly for huge amounts of money. Leeson told his bosses back in London that there was no risk, he was covered.

In all, Barings sent Nick Leeson more than a billion dollars, which was actually more than the bank was worth. Leeson said he was amazed that the money had been sent in the first place and then kept on coming. His consistent contention was that alarm bells should have gone off at the bank and someone should have stopped him. The problem was, he said, that the senior executives didn't know enough about derivatives to figure out what was going on.

Leeson in the Frankfurt airport

HIGH-RISK DERIVATIVES

If Barings executives were mystified by derivatives, they were not alone. The same year that Nick Leeson brought down the bank, Steve Kroft reported on these "highly exotic, little understood, virtually unregulated" securities. The derivatives market was worth $35 trillion worldwide, yet almost no one could explain what they were. Kroft said it was a story "too complicated to explain, but too important to ignore."

Kroft told how Orange County, California, had gone bankrupt after $1.7 billion of taxpayers' money had gone down the drain on derivatives. The county treasurer, a "highly sophisticated institutional investor," said he didn't understand what he was buying.

Steve Kroft gamely explained how derivatives worked. Or tried to. It is an agreement whose value derives from something else, which could be something simple like the future price of corn or wheat or some extremely complex note that would pay interest depending on lots of variable factors. There were more than 1,200 types of the things, created by mathematicians and physicists and calculated on computers.

Derivatives were characterized by their extreme volatility. The list of institutions that had lost heavily with them was long: Procter and Gamble, the Minneapolis Symphony Orchestra, the City Colleges of Chicago, the Eastern Shoshone Tribe of Wyoming, and a host of small communities like Auburn, Maine, and Painesville, Ohio. And Barings Bank.

::

Barings' auditors finally wised up and began moving in on Leeson. On February 23, 1995, Leeson faxed his resignation to the bank, apologizing for the mess he'd left, and said he was on the verge of a breakdown. He headed off with his wife, Lisa, for a vacation on the island of Borneo. For three days, he was oblivious to what was going on. Then he saw a newspaper story about the collapse of a bank. It was Barings. Figuring Nick might face a long jail term in a Southeast Asian jail, the Leesons flew back to Europe. On the plane, he saw people reading newspaper stories about Barings with pictures of him alongside. He slumped down in his seat and tried to hide his face under a baseball cap.

When he got to Frankfurt, the German authorities, rather than send Leeson to the U.K., worked to extradite him back to Singapore, where he faced fourteen years in the infamously unappetizing Changi Prison. On the BBC, David Frost asked Leeson, who was waiting to hear his fate, if he considered himself a criminal, a rogue trader, or just a trader who had had some bad luck. Leeson said he had to be a criminal because he was in jail. He agreed that he was a rogue trader. His insistent contention was that he wasn't a thief. What many people couldn't believe was Leeson's assertion that he hadn't stolen any of the money and hidden it somewhere.

::

From jail in Germany, Nick Leeson said that officials at Barings had never really bothered to check and see what he was doing. Neither had the Bank of England used its regulatory power to

JOHN RUSNAK

Nick Leeson told David Frost that this wasn't the first time something like this had happened, nor would it be the last. Leeson's prediction seemed to be confirmed in 2002, when a trader at Allied Irish Banks' Baltimore-based Allfirst Financial subsidiary was accused of trying to cover up losses of $691 million in foreign currency deals. Like Nick Leeson, John Rusnak had gambled, in his case that the yen would weaken against the dollar. When it hadn't, he had allegedly covered up his losses.

Neither AIB nor Allfirst was taken down as Barings had been. Indeed, AIB reported a large profit for 2001. The parent company fired its auditors and restructured its management to try to make sure the loss of controls wouldn't be repeated. In June 2002, Rusnak was indicted by a federal grand jury on charges that included bank fraud and false entry in bank records.

Prosecutors said Rusnak hadn't profited from the trading losses himself, but he had manipulated the bank's records to make it seem as if it were making money so he could qualify for performance-related bonuses. U.S. Attorney Thomas M. DiBiagio said that Rusnak had earned more than $850,000 in five years, $550,000 of it in bonuses. Rusnak faced up to thirty years in prison, a $1 million fine, and five years of probation for each of seven counts.

review his activities. What was left of Barings, which had once been called the sixth power of Europe, was subsequently sold to a Dutch group, ING, for £1, which at the time was worth about $1.60.

::

Nick Leeson eventually served three and a half years of a six-and-a-half-year sentence for fraud in Singapore. When he was released in 1999, he'd nearly died from cancer he was diagnosed with while in jail, his wife had divorced him, and he was faced with enormous debts to Barings' creditors, £850 million of whose money he had lost.

Leeson went on to write a book called *Rogue Trader* that was made into a movie starring Ewan McGregor. He started giving lectures—in 1999, it was reported that a Dutch business conference paid him $100,000 to talk about world stock markets. Most of the money he made went to the bank's creditors.

In 2000, Leeson got in trouble again when he was arrested in the United Kingdom for driving with three times the legal limit of alcohol in his system. He was moving his car so it wouldn't be clamped while he was watching his favorite soccer team on TV in a bar.

In 2001, Leeson told the London *Guardian* newspaper that he was getting about $5,000 a month from his frozen assets. Again, he rejected persistent stories that he had Barings money stashed away somewhere. He said he'd been offered a job doing risk management by an energy-trading firm in the Netherlands. Leeson said he was well qualified. He'd broken every risk and compliance rule there was, so who better to police the regulations than him?

Bill Stoecker

Whiz Kid

:: July 8, 1990 ::

In 1990, Ed Bradley met Bill Stoecker, another young man who was experiencing serious money problems at a bank. Stoecker had falsely obtained huge amounts of money. He had borrowed it for himself and used the money to buy whole companies and finance his lavish lifestyle. He had obtained perhaps half a billion dollars in all—and much of it was borrowed, backed by no collateral whatsoever.

In the late 1970s, Stoecker dropped out of college and started borrowing money to fix up houses that banks had foreclosed on. He thought he had stumbled on a good plan. If people could borrow money to buy houses, he thought, why couldn't they do so to buy companies? Stoecker persuaded some of the country's most prestigious financial institutions to lend him money, bankrolling a brief but spectacular run. At the height of his success, Stoecker was a hero in his hometown of Oak Forest, Illinois, giving millions of dollars to the community college he had left after one semester and tens of thousands of dollars to his high school, where he had played football. The *Chicago Tribune* called him the "Oak Forest Whiz Kid."

Bill Stoecker and Ed Bradley

The list of banks that lent Stoecker money was impressive. Representatives from the Bank of New England met him and three weeks later lent him $6 million with no collateral. The bank eventually headed a syndicate that lent Stoecker $150 million. Bankers Trust was in for $50 million, Citibank about $100 million. Ed Bradley asked Stoecker about that initial $6 million from the Bank of New England:

Bill Stoecker: "That is extremely rare—extremely exciting for an entrepreneur, I might add—but extremely aggressive for a bank."

Ed Bradley: "So they gave you six million dollars with nothing to secure it? Nothing you put up as collateral?"

Stoecker: "Unsecured, yeah. At that time."
Bradley: "Six million bucks?"
Stoecker: "Six million bucks."
Bradley: "That's pretty heady!"
Stoecker: "Yeah, we thought it was real interesting."

As far as the banks were concerned, Stoecker was a hugely successful businessman. He had a very large house in Chicago and two lavish getaways in Naples, Florida, with extravagant complexes of palm tree–lined pools. He had bodyguards, a stretch Mercedes, private jets and helicopters, and an art collection he valued at $13 million. Part of his collection was made up of old British hunting art, pictures of noblemen riding to hounds and other baronial pursuits. This was the kind of taste that impressed some members of the financial community.

Before he turned thirty, Stoecker's accountants figured he had enough money to be counted as one of the two hundred richest people in America.

But the whole financial edifice was a house of cards. Tom Raleigh, the attorney in charge of liquidating Stoecker's estate, said that Stoecker had been repaying one loan with another. As he described it, it was "just basically a very sophisticated check-kiting scheme."

Lee Seidler of Wall Street investment bank Bear Stearns explained that Stoecker had gone about establishing his business in an intelligent way. He built up a good credit rating by taking loans from local banks and paying them off in good time. The loans got larger and larger, and eventually the banks came to him for business. Seidler, laughing, said he knew this wasn't everyone's image of a bank. Ed Bradley agreed—he thought it was difficult to get money from a banker.

Lee Seidler: "It's only hard to get money from a banker if you're a little guy trying to get a little home mortgage, because, after all, you're just a little retail customer. But think big, and that's exactly what Stoecker was doing."

Stoecker's Grabill Corporation owned about two dozen companies, mostly in the Midwest. Some of the companies were real manufacturing operations: One made firearms; another, bodies for tow trucks; a third, the caps worn by Chicago police officers. But most of the firms weren't profitable, and Stoecker had no interest in actually managing them. He was just good at borrowing the money.

Stoecker looked great on paper. His accounting firm, Laventhol and Horwath, said his real estate was worth $74 million, his stocks were worth $220 million, and his personal fortune exceeded $500 million. But Tom Raleigh said that Stoecker was paying the accountants the unheard-of fee of $185,000 a month. Raleigh said when you are paid that kind of money, you don't ask too many difficult questions.

Ed Bradley: "You think he was a con man?"
Tom Raleigh: "Absolutely. Of the highest order. The financial statements are simply incredible. I think he sat down with a PC and just created out of whole cloth a lot of these financial statements."

The man who allegedly created this fictitious financial empire looked, if possible, even younger than Nick Leeson did when he was bringing down Barings Bank. With his hair down to his shirt collar, he might have been taken for a high school senior, not a business mogul. But Stoecker was no pushover. He strongly resisted Ed Bradley's attempts to get him to admit to any wrong-doing.

Take the evaluations of his companies, which it was alleged that Stoecker had simply made up. Stoecker told Ed Bradley that it's the auditor's job to verify your figures. But it seemed that Laventhol and Horwath hadn't checked anything when it valued Stoecker's Chandler Enterprises, which Stoecker was offering as collateral for a loan, at $63 million.

The company was described as a "diverse manufacturing and machining house." At the time he said that, Stoecker contested, it would have had to have been true. But in a separate court deposition, Stoecker stated that Chandler was not an operating company or a manufacturing company—in effect that, for practical purposes, Chandler Enterprises didn't exist. Ed Bradley asked Stoecker directly which it was. Either the company was worth something, or it wasn't. Stoecker said he really wasn't interested which it was. "Be honest with me, Bill," Bradley implored, but Stoecker merely said he didn't know what was the truth.

Eventually, Chandler was one of five companies valued collectively by Laventhol and Horwath at $232 million whose actual worth was close to zero.

Ed Bradley: "So they didn't really do anything, these companies? They didn't manufacture anything?"

Bill Stoecker: "No. If you're asking me if these companies were, for all intents and purposes, nonoperating entities, used as acquiring vehicles, or whatever, you're essentially correct."

Bradley wondered why Stoecker hadn't told the banks of the discrepancy between the stated value of the companies that he was using as collateral and their true worth. It was, after all, a lie. Indignantly, Stoecker said the banks hadn't known anything about the companies until six months after they'd made their last loan. As far as he was concerned, the companies were a nonissue.

::

Neither the accountants nor the Bank of New England wanted to talk about their involvement with Stoecker. Stoecker told Ed Bradley it had taken *60 Minutes* just a day or two to figure out what was going on, so the bankers and accountants should have been able to find out, too. Bankers are traditionally the most skeptical people on Earth, he said, and an auditor's sole function is to verify your financial statements and not take your word for them. Now everybody was saying that Stoecker was the reincarnation of evil, but they had so many opportunities to look at his activities. "How stupid can these people be?" he asked. Rather than accept blame himself, Stoecker wanted others to be held responsible for not stopping him.

As far as the banks were concerned, Tom Raleigh said it was the young MBAs who had been taken in. Older guys had asked tougher questions. One said he had sat down with Stoecker over after-dinner drinks and cigars. He asked, "How do you make money?" and Stoecker couldn't answer. That's when the official knew there was a problem.

The Bank of New England finally forced Stoecker into bankruptcy in 1989, after he defaulted on a loan payment and they realized a lot of his assets didn't really exist. All Stoecker's genuine assets were seized, and the banks filed a claim against him for fraud. Stoecker had already been indicted for allegedly lying to the bankruptcy trustee, Tom Raleigh. Ed Bradley asked Raleigh about Stoecker's ability to tell the truth.

Tom Raleigh: "I don't believe that he knows what the truth is at this point. I think that Bill Stoecker has conned himself. He believes his own lies at this point."

For his part, Bill Stoecker thought that if he had to go to jail, the bankers and accountants and attorneys should, too. Laventhol and Horwath said it had been a victim as well and paid $30 million to the banks. The Bank of New England wrote off $65 million of its loans to Stoecker. Stoecker himself was acquitted in a trial for bankruptcy fraud.

::

In 1997, it was reported that Stoecker, then forty, had been convicted on numerous counts of bank fraud, making false statements to financial institutions, and giving or receiving bribes in exchange for procuring loans. He was sentenced to ninety months' imprisonment, to be followed by three years of supervised release and no less than $121,652,607 in restitution. He appealed his conviction and sentence, but in June 2000 the U.S. Court of Appeals upheld the conviction. Bill Stoecker is serving his time in the federal prison in Oxford, Wisconsin, and his scheduled release date is June 19, 2004.

Daniel Teyibo

A Free Ride

:: January 24, 1994 ::

In 1994, Ed Bradley met a man who had helped himself to a free ride on the financial markets. With so many large deals made electronically, over the phone or by fax, dealers often buy and sell from people they have never been introduced to in person or even seen. The kind of trust that large financial transactions require on both sides often has to be established over the telephone. If someone calls and says he is from a particular brokerage firm and he sounds convincing, he might be able to work a deal. This is what Daniel Teyibo did on numerous occasions in the course of perpetrating what may have been the largest free-riding scam in the history of the Treasuries market.

Daniel Teyibo did business with about twenty-five Wall Street brokerage houses, making bond deals that may have totaled a billion dollars. Teyibo would call the trading desk of a large firm directly and claim to be a big player. Which he wasn't. Willie Daniels, founder of the United Daniels brokerage house, was one of the people Teyibo failed to con. Daniels said Teyibo was up-to-date on everything; he knew what he wanted and sounded just like a trader from a major New York house. As Daniels said, as long as the dollar amounts look good, people will make the trade.

One of the first people to catch Teyibo out was Robert McDonough of Merrill Lynch. McDonough told Ed Bradley that Teyibo had called him wanting to buy $500 million worth of Treasuries. If the market went in his favor for one day, Teyibo could take the free ride. If a customer closes out a transaction by the end of the day, he doesn't actually have to have the money, McDonough explained. You have to hope against hope that the market goes up so you can sell and keep the difference. But if things don't go its way, the customer could be stuck with the loss.

::

Ed Bradley showed up at Daniel Teyibo's house to talk to him about his work. At first Teyibo was reluctant, but he decided to meet with Bradley, and he changed into a smart double-breasted business suit for the purpose. Teyibo and Bradley sat on a couch and looked over records of Teyibo's big-money transactions. Teyibo explained how he had leveraged his deals and how easy it had been for him to get money. To buy a security, he would go to the repo market, which allows traders to buy bonds and get a loan to pay for them using the same bonds as collateral. In this way Teyibo was able to borrow $9 million for just $799.

But a company such as Goldman Sachs has its capital, which

Daniel Teyibo and Bradley

acts as collateral. Ed Bradley ascertained that Teyibo would have needed a lot of fake documentation—false financial statements—to pull off these deals. The company selling to him would have to have believed Teyibo had enough money to pay back the loan.

Most of these esoteric financial transactions are made by men in white shirts and ties sitting in front of flashing computer screens in loud, hectic open-plan office floors. It is an obscure world with its own language and cryptic practices. Ed Bradley asked Daniel Teyibo where his office was. Teyibo said it was in his basement. He took Bradley downstairs and showed off his office. In a badly lit room with unfinished concrete walls was a jumble of computer equipment. Using satellite and modem links, Teyibo could get access to all the financial information he needed from anywhere in the world.

When he made his calls from his basement, Teyibo would apparently often use a fake name. Court documents showed he had used names such as Jack Renfro, Paul Palmer, and Richard Gant. In February 1992, a man called Jack Renfro called the

Dean Witter office in New York, claiming to be a trader from its office in Chevy Chase, Maryland. Renfro wanted to execute a $5 million trade for a client. Dean Witter taped the conversation. Part of the tape was played on the broadcast. At the end, Renfro was told, "You are done at five million long bonds at 1026."

After doing the deal, the trader got suspicious because he couldn't find any Jack Renfro listed in the Chevy Chase office. He called "Renfro," who explained that because he'd just started there, he wasn't in the system yet. But Dean Witter said it wouldn't continue to deal with Renfro. The broker then got a call from a man named Richard Gant, who said that Jack Renfro worked for him.

Dean Witter caught on, confronted Gant about Renfro, and cut him off. Gant said that Dean Witter owed him money, but a supervisor advised him to desist. He said he had everything on tape. "You're not authorized to execute a trade against me," the supervisor said firmly. "You're out."

Dean Witter contended that Daniel Teyibo would call using different voices and accents. Teyibo said they really were different people. *60 Minutes* analyzed Dean Witter tapes of Renfro and Gant and Ed Bradley's interview of Teyibo and found that the voices almost definitely belonged to the same person. When Ed Bradley asked Teyibo about this, he had a novel explanation for the impersonations:

Ed Bradley: "After they were analyzed, Teyibo admitted that he had passed himself off as both Richard Gant and Jack Renfro. His explanation? Richard Gant had told him to."

As for Paul Palmer, Teyibo said he was in Africa. Apparently Palmer used to be known as Sir Paul Palmer. But that wasn't because he'd received a knighthood from Queen Elizabeth, Teyibo said; Palmer just used the title "sir." Also in Africa, according to Teyibo, was a Samuel Stein of the Stein & Stein Company, which the Securities and Exchange Commission said Teyibo had created. But there was no trace of either "Stein" or "Palmer." Or the second Stein of Stein & Stein, for that matter. Teyibo was unable to put *60 Minutes* in touch with any of these people or any of his business associates in the United States or Africa.

Daniel Teyibo insisted to Ed Bradley that he was not a crook. He said he was "just a very knowledgeable investor, someone that you can call a sophisticated investor." He was "an honest businessman."

Four days after his interview with Ed Bradley, Daniel Teyibo was charged with seventeen counts of securities fraud. He was in jail awaiting his day in court when the program aired.

::

In March 1994, Mike Wallace reported that the SEC had won a $923,000 judgment against Daniel Teyibo, and he had also been indicted for securities and wire fraud. If found guilty, he would face ten years in jail.

In March 1995, Daniel Teyibo was convicted. He served nineteen months in prison and was released to the Immigration and Naturalization Service in October 1996. He was deported back to Nigeria soon after.

Edward Reiners and John Ruffo

The $353 Million Con

:: February 21, 1999 ::

In February 1999, Steve Kroft reported on a massive bank fraud, one of the largest in U.S. history. What was unusual about this particular con was the possibility that one of the two men involved had gotten away with it. As the program went on the air, Edward Reiners was safely behind bars, but his former partner, John Ruffo, was on the run. He had disappeared with some unintentional assistance from federal authorities, who appeared to have been the victims of his final con.

For twenty years, Ed Reiners had worked at Philip Morris, where one of his jobs was to approve the buying and leasing of computers. Reiners bought some of his equipment from John Ruffo, a computer dealer in New York City. In 1993, Reiners was let go by Philip Morris. In the spring of that year, the two longtime business associates had lunch at a Manhattan restaurant. Reiners

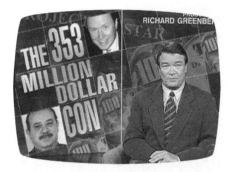

Steve Kroft reporting on Reiners's and Ruffo's scam

was thinking about getting another job; Ruffo talked about his dreams of making millions in the stock market.

The two men began by talking about regular business opportunities. Eventually the conversation got around to a different kind of idea, one that adapted the business relationship they'd established: What if they went to a bank and borrowed money to buy computers but put it into the stock market instead? Almost as soon

John Ruffo

as the idea was articulated, the two men were working the con.

Reiners, with his long experience at Philip Morris, was the front man. He pretended he still worked there, on something called Project Star. Reiners and Ruffo put together a package of documents and approached the banks. Edward Reiners told Steve Kroft that they had said Project Star involved highly secret research on and development of smokeless cigarettes. The research was purportedly being conducted at five offshore locations that needed staff and computers. The project was so secret that the men said they couldn't reveal the final destinations of the computers, or even their serial numbers.

Reiners and Ruffo drew up a confidentiality agreement that said the bankers could talk only to Reiners. They'd be sued if they contacted Philip Morris. To Edward Reiners's surprise, they got their potential investors to sign it. Reiners told Steve Kroft he'd had a harder time getting a mortgage than persuading the bankers to put their names to his confidentiality agreement.

The two men approached Signet Bank, based in Richmond, Virginia, a city where Philip Morris had major operations. The bank had done other computer deals involving Ruffo and Reiners and expected to make millions of dollars in fees and interest on this one. Edward Reiners told Steve Kroft he didn't think they would get past the first presentation, one of numerous occasions on which Reiners was convinced they'd be found out. He assumed that someone would say they'd have to call the CFO, but it never happened. "They bought it," he said, as if he were still perplexed.

All they needed to close their deal was something called an incumbency certificate, an official document from Philip Morris giving Reiners the authority to conduct business on the company's behalf. An incumbency certificate is an official document that has to be embossed with the company seal and endorsed by a company officer. Reiners and Ruffo used the Yellow Pages to find a company in lower Manhattan that made official corporate stamps.

Edward Reiners: "We made up names of ten or twelve companies, told them we needed seals for CCS and WRE, other companies, and, by the way, Harold Morris, Philip Morris, and John Morris."

Steve Kroft: "So you had the whole Morris family."

Reiners: "Right. All the brothers."

Kroft: "And this worked?"

Reiners: "It worked, sir."

Having fabricated a certificate, the two men still needed the signature of a Philip Morris officer, preferably an obscure one. They picked an assistant corporate secretary named Diane McAdams from a list of officers. Reiners told Kroft he and Ruffo had been riding in a car in New York one day listening to the radio. The station had announced a giveaway—the tenth caller from the Bronx would win dinner for two at such-and-such restaurant. This gave them an idea.

They called Diane McAdams, saying they were from WPLJ in New York, and told her she'd won dinner at an expensive restaurant. She was very happy about it. Before she got her prize, however, she was told, she'd have to sign a release form. Reiners and Ruffo faxed her one. She signed it and faxed it back. Then they scanned her signature into a computer and reproduced it on the incumbency certificate. Reiners told Steve Kroft they had kept their part of the bargain and sent McAdams a voucher for the dinner.

John Reiners

When he went to present the certificate, Reiners thought he'd be grilled about it for hours, but the loan officer accepted the document and said, "Let's go to lunch." With that, the first installment of $25 million was wired into John Ruffo's company account.

Other institutions joined, until seven foreign and domestic banks had invested in Project Star. The crazy-sounding idea hatched over an innocuous lunch, an idea that was buttressed by little more than the two men's wits, garnered more than $353 million from the banks. Everything was sealed up by the confidentiality agreement. No one ever asked to see a computer. Of course, as Edward Reiners admitted, there were no computers.

::

Ruffo and Reiners could simply have run off with the money. But that would have seemed like common theft. They decided to play the stock market with it, thereby fulfilling the fantasy Ruffo had told Reiners about over lunch. If they could make the loan repayments with their gains, no one would ask any questions and they could eventually retire. With all that money, the two men were big players in the market.

From jail, Ed Reiners, looking a little gaunt, talked about working the stock market with hundreds of millions of dollars to play with. Reiners recalled that the biggest position they had held was 2.2 million shares of Texas Instruments, worth about $90 million. With that kind of capital, the two men were very popular on Wall Street. The two men visited the floor of the New York Stock Exchange and were wined and dined by the brokers. One firm alone made $6 million in a year in commissions on their trades.

Reiners bought a $3 million penthouse in Trump Palace in Manhattan, but every time the phone rang he thought it could be the end. He said it was a very edgy, very draining existence. In March 1996, a Japanese bank got curious, called Philip Morris, and found that Reiners didn't work there. The bank demanded a face-to-face meeting.

Reiners and Ruffo tried a desperate last-minute ruse. Through an old friend, Reiners borrowed a conference room at Philip Morris and used one of Ruffo's employees to play the part of Diane McAdams to try to talk the bank around. But the bank had tipped off the FBI, and the Bureau listened in on the meeting. Reiners said they'd had no choice at that point but to try to save the scheme. The only alternative was to run.

Both men were arrested after the meeting. Ed Reiners confessed and was sentenced to more than sixteen years in prison, despite the fact that he had helped recover more than $200 million of the money, most of it from Ruffo's investment accounts. Reiners and Ruffo no longer had $353 million to return. In a period of growth in the market, Ruffo and Reiners had managed to lose $70 million. John Klein, the assistant U.S. attorney who prosecuted the case, said, "They bucked a trend." When it came to playing the market, they weren't as good as they thought they were.

The government spent a year building its case against John Ruffo and indicted him on 160 counts of bank fraud and money laundering. Just before his trial, Ruffo pled guilty to all counts in exchange for an agreement that allowed him to stay free on $10 million bail until he was ordered to surrender.

On the morning of November 9, 1998, Ruffo reported as directed to the Federal District Courthouse in Brooklyn to hand over his electronic monitoring bracelet. He was then given four hours to surrender himself to Fairton Federal Prison in New Jersey. He never showed up. John Klein admitted they could have had the judge lock him up after sentencing. Steve Kroft asked him if he wished he had.

John Klein: "Well, it's unfortunate that Mr. Ruffo did not self-surrender. It's unfortunate that Mr. Ruffo did not keep his promise to the court. It's unfortunate that he lied about his intentions to self-surrender."

Steve Kroft: "But he's a con man."

John Klein: "He is now a fugitive. That's a temporary circumstance. The government will remedy that circumstance. We will find him."

Klein said that some of the money, maybe more than $13 million, was still unaccounted for.

Ruffo left what was apparently a suicide note for his wife, Linda. But she didn't believe for a minute that he'd killed himself. She said she believed her husband was innocent. She didn't even know he was supposed to report to jail. When she'd first heard the charges against him, she'd made her husband get down on his knees and, as she put it, "beat him up." He swore he hadn't done anything. Linda Ruffo told Steve Kroft that the couple had no money and that his mother had been giving him $40 a week just to get by on.

Linda Ruffo: "At what point in time were we going to enjoy this so-called money they say we had?"
Steve Kroft: "Your husband may be enjoying it now."
Ruffo: "No. I know that he's not."

To secure the $10 million bail bond, Linda Ruffo pledged her house, both their mothers' houses, and some uncles' and aunts' houses. Since her husband had run away, Linda Ruffo and the relatives, most of whom were over seventy, were now homeless.

Linda Ruffo: "What upset the family more than anything, and of course myself, is that for two years, the government labeled my husband a criminal, put a tag on his ankle,

called him a flight risk for two years, took his passport
away, took my passport away, yet they cut the band off
his ankle on November ninth and said, 'Good-bye, go to
jail on your own?' And now they tell you, 'Tough luck,
you put up your homes'?"

Edward Reiners figured John Ruffo could have anywhere from $8
to $15 million. "The world's a big place," he said, "he could be
anywhere." Ruffo had always dreamed of living in a villa in Italy,
retiring there to drink the good wine he loved. Steve Kroft said
Ruffo had the perfect, unmemorable face for a villain. He had
hair receding over the top of his roundish head and sported a
mustache in the pictures of him that were shown. He could be
anywhere. Kroft said he and the crew thought they'd seen him at
a Wendy's in Queens the week before the broadcast.

Jeffrey Lichtman was Ruffo's last lawyer. Steve Kroft asked if
he thought the authorities would find his client.

Jeffrey Lichtman: "That's a tough question. I think that if I had
to be a betting man, I'd put my money on John Ruffo."
Steve Kroft: "Why?"
Lichtman: "Because from what I can see so far, he's smarter than
the people looking for him."

Perhaps John Ruffo never made it to his dream villa in Italy. In
April 2001, the U.S. Marshals Service issued a warning that
Ruffo had recently been to several banks in the more prosaic loca-
tion of Duncan, Oklahoma, and tried to make a wire transfer.

Ruffo had asked to see the bank president and said he wanted to set up an account to receive wire transfers of large sums of money from Nigeria. The money was coming from finder's fees he was earning as a liquidator, he said. Ruffo hadn't succeeded in setting up an account. According to the U.S. marshals, who have Ruffo on their "Fifteen Most Wanted" list, he had used his real name.

The Ultimate Con Man

:: January 1, 1989 ::

All of the con men *60 Minutes* has met over the years were success-ful, at least for a time. They wouldn't have been newsworthy if they hadn't been. Some were spectacularly good at what they did, but only one, by definition, could be "the Ultimate Con Man." In 1989, that accolade was bestowed on Dr. John Ackah Blay-Miezah of Ghana, and no one has since emerged to knock him from the pedestal. At his peak, Blay-Miezah was nothing less than the rich-est man in the world, worth a staggering $27 billion. At least that's what he said.

Dr. Blay-Miezah went by a number of names. To his fellow Ghanaians, he was known as Nana Ackah Nyanzu II. To others, he was "the Fat Man" or just "Doc." In 1989, Dr. Blay-Miezah was living and running his operation in London in considerable style. He managed to maintain a lavish lifestyle despite the fact that his massive fortune lay tantalizingly out of his reach. Of the $27 billion, he had access to not one cent.

The problem was that the billions were tied up in a secret trust fund of which Blay-Miezah was the sole beneficiary. The trust was so secret and complex that he needed financial help to unlock the funds. The richest man in the world had to get people to invest in him personally to help him realize his vast fortune. To attract investors, Dr. Blay-Miezah promised people a return of not less than 1,000 percent on their money. That meant a $1 million loan would be transformed into a $10 million payment.

The promise of these returns proved irresistible to hundreds of Americans. Blay-Miezah's story had worked, and around the world, it was estimated, he had attracted $250 million to help him gain access to his billions. Of the $250 million, about $200 million had been provided by Americans.

Ed Bradley spoke with some of the people who had found Blay-Miezah's blandishments too enticing to refuse. Barry Ginsburg, a lawyer from Philadelphia, said that friends of his had basically been throwing money at him after he told them the story and said he was giving Blay-Miezah money. Ginsburg and his friends handed over nearly $2 million. Walter Hajduk, a businessman from New Jersey, met Blay-Miezah through friends in Philadelphia, where Doc had started his operation. When Ed Bradley mentioned to Hajduk that he'd heard he might have put up $7 million over the years, Hajduk didn't wave him off that figure. He just said he'd made a "considerable" investment. He had seen not a penny in return.

Dr. Blay-Miezah's extraordinary story was obviously convincingly told. Walter Hajduk said he thought the man spoke with sincerity. Hajduk looked Blay-Miezah in the eye, and Doc told him what the money was for. Barry Ginsburg recalled telling his father, "'Dad, it's so outrageous.' I mean, how can you concoct a story like his?"

::

The source of Dr. Blay-Miezah's colossal fortune was, he claimed, Kwame Nkrumah, the first president of the Republic of Ghana. The story was that over the ten years of his rule, which ended when he was deposed in 1966, Nkrumah had smuggled tons of gold and enormous proceeds from Ghana's cocoa industry out of the country and into Swiss bank accounts. He had then set up the Oman Ghana Trust and made John Ackah Blay-Miezah its sole beneficiary. On various occasions, Blay-Miezah said he was the son or nephew or cousin of Nkrumah. He often told investors how close he was to Kwame Nkrumah. He was so close, he said, that he had been there at the bedside when Nkrumah had died in exile in Romania in 1972.

That part of the story was simple to refute. Blay-Miezah couldn't have been in Romania in 1972 with his dying presidential benefactor, as he was actually in Graterford Prison in Pennsylvania serving a one-to-two-year sentence for posing as a U.N. diplomat and defrauding a Philadelphia hotel out of the more earthbound sum of $2,000.

::

Ed Bradley talked with Dr. Blay-Miezah in his extravagant quarters in London. Someone let Bradley in through the cast-iron gates of a very large London home that had a white Rolls-Royce in the driveway. Another man opened the front door and then went to help Dr. Blay-Miezah carry out what he said was an old tribal custom, one that meant he was vowing to speak the truth. The custom as performed for the camera seemed to consist of daubing Beefeater gin on his throne and spitting at his scepter three times. Blay-Miezah was dressed in traditional African clothing and seated on a gilt-edged throne for the interview, and the conversation continued in the splendid formal garden of the home.

Bradley was naturally interested in Blay-Miezah's assertions that investors would see some return on their money. Although none had in fourteen years. Blay-Miezah insisted that no one was being defrauded. The Oman Ghana Fund was real and contained billions of dollars. People would be paid, he insisted. He guaranteed it.

Ed Bradley: "Well, what is the guarantee?"
Dr. Blay-Miezah: "Mr. Bradley, my word is better than my bond. When I promise you that if you give me $100,000, I'll give you $1 million, I will never, never, never, never dishonor it."
Bradley: "That's your word."
Blay-Miezah: "That is my word. And it—"
Bradley: "Better than your bond."
Blay-Miezah: "—oh, yes."

Dr. Blay-Miezah worked out of the offices of the Oman Ghana Trust in London's expensive Piccadilly. He arrived there each day in his white Rolls-Royce flanked by a bevy of serious-looking private British security guards. Much of Blay-Miezah's workday consisted of reassuring his anxious investors that he was busy trying to release the billions of dollars in the trust. He told a group of people sitting in his office that he'd been branded a confidence man and a flimflam artist over the years, but he hadn't defrauded anybody. He earnestly contended that the only reason they hadn't been paid was the difficulty he was having in clearing the blockages.

Blay-Miezah had attracted investors with dozens of documents to back up his claims. Oman Ghana Trust brochures listed more than twenty subsidiary companies that would help develop Ghana once the money was released. Investors were kept on the hook with a range of excuses from military coups in Ghana to the overcautious nature of Swiss bankers.

As Ed Bradley explained, if anyone got too suspicious or asked too many questions, the amount of the ultimate payoff would simply be raised. Barry Ginsburg, for one, confronted Blay-Miezah, asking him when he'd get his money. Ginsburg told Bradley that Blay-Miezah had said he'd write a new figure down on a piece of paper. If Ginsburg didn't like it, he should say so. The figure was $150 million.

Ginsburg said he felt very good, he thought the episode was coming to a close, and he would be getting his money any day. But nothing happened. By 1986, he had had enough and filed a complaint with the district attorney's office in Philadelphia. He claimed that Blay-Miezah and his American associate Robert Ellis had defrauded him and a group of investors of nearly $2 million. Ellis was tried and convicted and sentenced to a minimum of five years in prison. A warrant was issued for Blay-Miezah's arrest.

Philadelphia district attorney Ronald Castille explained that Blay-Miezah's network of companies existed only on paper and was a prop, just like the Rolls-Royces, the palaces, the tribal robes, and the retinue of retainers. Blay-Miezah was shown presiding over a function at which people sat watching a tribal dance. Doc sat regally, looking on in his African finery. These were all top-drawer examples of what Mel Weinberg had called "fruit salad." Blay-Miezah's whole edifice was just an extraordinarily elaborate confidence game, as far as the DA was concerned.

By the time a warrant was issued for his arrest, Blay-Miezah had long since fled the United States and moved back to Ghana. But he was picked up by the authorities in his home country, and he was facing a lot more than jail time. Blay-Miezah was charged with economic crimes against the state, charges which in Ghana carried the death penalty. But Ronald Castille said that Blay-Miezah was such a confidence man, he was able to convince the Ghanaian authorities to let him go and it was then that he moved on to London so he could work on distributing the fund. As Castille put it, Blay-Miezah had talked himself off of death row.

Blay-Miezah showed up in London accompanied by an unlikely traveling partner: the man who had arrested him in Ghana. Ed Bradley met the man and tried to determine whether Blay-Miezah had talked him into working for the trust or whether he was keeping an eye on his former charge for the authorities. The man told Bradley that he was with the police but was also working as an assistant for Dr. Blay-Miezah in his office. He was working for both Blay-Miezah and the government, he said.

Indeed, Dr. Blay-Miezah had somehow become an official of

the government of the Republic of Ghana. He was not a minister as such, he said, but he was instructed to do special duties—special duties that related to the fund. Whatever the job entailed, the key point was that his position with the government was legitimate enough that Dr. Blay-Miezah enjoyed diplomatic immunity in the United Kingdom. He couldn't be arrested there or extradited to the United States. The condition the Ghanaian government attached to his status was that Kwame Nkrumah's name be left out of future discussions of the trust.

So when Ed Bradley interviewed Dr. Blay-Miezah in London, his line now was that the former president had had no involvement at all in the fund. That had been little more than a rumor. The complicated setup involving the president and the smuggled gold and cocoa profits had gone away completely.

Ed Bradley: "I'm totally confused."
Dr. Blay-Miezah: "Oh yes, you should be."
Bradley: "Where did the money in the fund come from?"
Blay-Miezah: "From our—from our ancestors."
Bradley: "From your ancestors?"
Blay-Miezah: "Ancestors, yes."
Bradley: "Where did they get so much money?"
Blay-Miezah: "Where did they get the money from? Well, I cannot disclose it."

Dr. Blay-Miezah's game had nearly been up on another occasion some years before. In 1979, he had been sentenced to seven years in prison in Ghana for fraud and bribery of government officials.

He had been saved that time by a truly unlikely hero, one of the most prominent figures in America's biggest political scandal, Watergate. Former U.S. Attorney General John Mitchell, who was no stranger to jail himself, had flown to Ghana and persuaded the government to release Blay-Miezah.

In London, Ed Bradley asked Doc what relationship he had had with Mitchell. He was told that Mitchell was an adviser. He hadn't invested any money, but, as the saying goes, time is money. Blay-Miezah said that Mitchell had put in a lot of time; time that was worth "more than billions." When the Philadelphia DA heard exactly how much money, he had a comment:

Ronald Castille: "And what will he get for this time that he's put in? A handsome settlement of—"

Ed Bradley: "$733 million is the figure I saw."

Castille: "This is what Mitchell's going to get? [*Laughs*] That's the big roll of the dice right there. I wonder what that makes for an hourly rate? I wonder if that's above scale?"

John Mitchell died in November 1988 and never saw his money, either billions or millions. The people who had put their money into Blay-Miezah's scheme were left to sit and wait. For Walter Hajduk, waiting had become his way of life. He was filmed smoking a cigarette in a room at the Oman Ghana Trust office. He told Ed Bradley he'd been called a fool, been called crazy. People said the Fat Man was boiling him in a pot, pouring salt in. The guy was having him for dinner. Ed Bradley asked how much of his $7 million investment he expected to see back. At that point, Hajduk said, it wasn't the money, it was satisfaction he wanted—satisfaction that he had been right. He looked worn out.

Ed Bradley: "When it's all over, what will you say?"
Walter Hajduk: "Hooray."

But John Ackah Blay-Miezah told Ed Bradley in London in September 1988 that he had some good news. He'd heard from his banks, and the funds were finally being released. He was very specific. He could start payments on the Wednesday of the week the interview took place. That was September 7, 1988. Blay-Miezah said that by the middle of November, "We should have finished with the Americans." Bradley noted that Blay-Miezah was busy drawing up lists of people to be paid. One list of Americans was due to be paid a total of more than $800 million. Of course, November came and went, and there was no sign of any money.

Ronald Castille had no doubts about Blay-Miezah's place in the pantheon of con men:

Ronald Castille: "This guy is good. He'll go down in history as a
   world-famous con man. This fraud has been going on
   for over fourteen years, perhaps even before that. It is of
   proportions that are unbelievable in the dollar figures,
   and it is worldwide. And this guy has fooled people from
   the heads of governments all the way down to a poor
   widow in the street."

Predictably, Dr. Blay-Miezah said that the DA was just plain wrong. He did not know him, he said. He wondered how many people in the world would be able to, as he put it, "drive this transaction" for eighteen years. Not a single person could. When Ed Bradley asked if he would ever go back to Philadelphia, Blay-Miezah asked why he shouldn't. He'd be able to prove that he was worth the billions of dollars he claimed that very week.

But in a call to *60 Minutes* two days before the piece aired in January 1989, Dr. Blay-Miezah said he was leaving London that weekend, not to return to the United States but to go to Ghana, where he would make preparations to meet all his obligations. Again he was quite precise: he'd be done by the end of the week. But at least four other times Blay-Miezah had gathered people together to pay their debts, and no one had ever received a penny.

Ed Bradley asked Ronald Castille if he ever expected to see Dr. Blay-Miezah back in the United States. "I'll be watching him on your show," he said. "That'll be about it."

::

60 Minutes revisited the story of John Ackah Blay-Miezah for "The Best of Cons" special in 1999. Ten years after the piece first aired, Blay-Miezah retained his prominence. Ed Bradley said of all the con men he had been involved with, Blay-Miezah was "clearly head and shoulders above the rest . . . the best con man I've ever seen in my life."

Bradley recalled that when he had first sat down with Blay-Miezah in London, he had been dressed like an affluent Western businessman in a Savile Row suit and a custom-made Charvet shirt from Paris with gold cuff links. Blay-Miezah asked if he could put on his ceremonial robes. Was it okay if he sat on his ceremonial throne? "Oh, you bet," Bradley had replied. In 1999, Ed Bradley gave Blay-Miezah a eulogy of sorts:

Ed Bradley: "Blay-Miezah was so good that today he's dead. He's been dead for, I don't know, five, six years now. His body was frozen in Geneva so that they could keep the fingerprints and everything intact. There are people still trying to get at the trust fund. . . . He was, without a doubt, the best of the best."

In mid-2002, Ghanaian news sources were reporting that efforts were being made to gain access to Oman Ghana Trust Fund money that was said to be held in Swiss bank accounts. The amount had ballooned to $42 billion. Even in death, Dr. Blay-Miezah was getting richer and richer.

Scamming Workers' Comp

:: April 12, 1992 ::

In addition to investigating individuals who might be involved in the kind of skullduggery described in this book, *60 Minutes* has also explored entire genres of scams. One was the widespread abuse of workers' compensation, the insurance employers are required to carry to cover medical bills for employees injured on the job. In 1992, Lesley Stahl looked into the legal and medical cons being perpetrated against the workers' comp system, cons which added up to a $3-billion-a-year rip-off.

The workers' comp scams are a true team effort. The worker will be taught how to fake an injury and file a claim for benefits. A lawyer will assist in the application for compensation for the supposed pain and suffering, and the symptoms will be treated by a sympathetic doctor. The money that can be made from fabricated injuries makes the scam worth the effort for the injured party, the

Don Burnett with Leslie Stahl

lawyers, and the doctors alike, but costly for the employer and their insurance provider.

Lesley Stahl spoke with a man who was trying to do something about it: Eugene Taylor, an insurance lawyer in Los Angeles. Taylor told Stahl about a man who cut his finger at work, a wound that required three stitches. Taylor laid his hand on top of a two-foot-high stack of paperwork. This was, he said, the medical portion of the man's file. This less-than-life-threatening injury had kept the man off work for three weeks. His medical bills were $37,000.

A workers' comp scam might typically originate outside an unemployment office like the one in Los Angeles where *60 Minutes* set up an undercover hidden camera operation. A woman, who was called Barbara for the purposes of the story, was primed to make a fraudulent claim against Don Burnett, a real-life businessman. Like Eugene Taylor, Don Burnett had a lot of manila files to show to Lesley Stahl. Burnett's files were full of phony workers' comp claims.

Burnett agreed to let Barbara pretend she had been working for him. The story was to be that Barbara had just been fired after working seven months in the meat-processing plant that he owned. Barbara wore a concealed microphone and went down to the unemployment office with her "boyfriend," who had a camera hidden in his cap.

Anyone hanging around an unemployment office might well be approached by someone known as a "capper," a go-between whose job it is to steer the mark to a lawyer's office, where the individual would be told he or she could squeeze more from workers' comp than they would be able to get on their own from unemployment. It didn't matter if the person was perfectly healthy, like Barbara.

Sure enough, Barbara was approached by a man who came up to her in the street before she reached her destination. The man asked Barbara if she'd been fired, and she said she had. The capper told Barbara she had no problem; he worked in workers' comp and he had a car waiting across the street. Barbara would do much better going with him to a lawyer than if she went over to the unemployment office.

Man: "Yeah, lawyer. You know, he give to you a lot of money, $350 for a week."

Barbara: "$350?"

Man: "Yes, yes, $350 a week."

Barbara and the "capper"

Barbara: "How much do I get if I go there?" [*Pointing toward the unemployment office*]

Man: "And there, you know, they give you maybe $79."

The capper gathered Barbara and her boyfriend and they set off for the lawyer's office. But there was one thing the capper had forgotten to find out.

Lesley Stahl: "On the way, he suddenly remembered: he never asked her what was wrong with her."

Man: "You know, you hurt your back? Something heavy, you know, something heavy—"

Barbara: "Well, I did computers, and I drove."

Man: "Yeah, yeah, no problem. Come on, let's go."

Eugene Taylor said that this capper could expect to make $450 for delivering a client to the law office Barbara was taken to. One group of cappers in Los Angeles, Taylor said, ran seven vans, and seven vans could generate a lot of money in a week.

Actually, it wasn't strictly necessary to run into a capper to find out about making a workers' comp claim. Eugene Taylor said that in Los Angeles an ad ran on television every six minutes from ten in the morning to ten at night telling people about workers' comp. Accompanied by poorly acted vignettes of the tensions of office life, the voiceover asked the viewers if they were suffering from stress on the job, or losing sleep; stomach problems or headaches; chest pains or depression? If so, they might be entitled to medical help and disability under workers' comp, "AT NO COST TO YOU!" as a message read on the screen. Lesley Stahl added that in California, all you have to do is prove that 10 percent of your stress comes from your job.

At the storefront law office she was taken to, Barbara, who was not aware she had any stress, work-related or otherwise, met a paralegal named Rosie. Rosie and Barbara met in a small office with heavy metal shutters over the windows. All over Rosie's desk were the kind of thick files and piles of papers that seemed to characterize this story. Once Barbara said that she used to drive from place to place setting up computer programs, Rosie knew what to say next.

Rosie: "And you can put it . . . a lower back injury."
Barbara: "Well, yeah, I—"
Rosie: "—by traveling . . . constant one position from traveling from places to places, you know."
Lesley Stahl: "Then Rosie opens up her full bag of symptoms—

symptoms that will generate medical exams and treatment. After all, that's where the money is."

Rosie: "Now, you're suffering neck, shoulder, and lower back
pain, because from driving, you know your shoulder . . .
you've got a stiff neck, okay. Then on the stress, you've
got stress, migraine headaches, you've got constant
headaches, blurred vision, because of constantly looking
at the computer, and anxiety . . . anxiety."

Barbara: "Anxiety."

Rosie: "You've got anxiety, nervousness, nightmares."

Rosie's diagnosis was the perfect example of Don Burnett's
nightmare. As he told Lesley Stahl, leafing through the papers
that he, as Barbara's supposed employer, had been sent, Barbara
wound up being sent to seven doctors to deal with all the ailments
that had been uncovered. Doctors that he would end up paying
for. Burnett had previously said he knew the buzzwords: stress,
lower back pain, pain that radiates down the right leg, and the
like. Areas where it is hard to come up with something that is
provable or not provable. And Barbara's injuries were indeed
described in those terms: pulled and strained muscles and lower
back pain.

Insurance companies have to pay for each separate medical
exam, so the scam would involve as many exams from as many
different doctors as possible, usually at places called "medical
mills." Lesley Stahl spoke with a chiropractor who used to work
at such a place. He said that a patient first sees a GP who would,
as he put it, "quote unquote, 'refer them'" to orthopedists and

neurologists and other specialists where the patient would be examined at every turn. An orthopedist might charge $800 to $1000 for such an exam, he said; a neurologist, $3000 if they administered the whole gamut of testing.

Barbara was tested by a psychiatrist and a chiropractor. Immediately, Barbara began receiving treatment with electrical patches attached to her back for what were diagnosed as a sprain, a strain, and a damaged tailbone, which the chiropractor identified after an exam that took one minute. Barbara was filmed lying on a bed in a medical office getting her treatment. The hidden camera also filmed a woman saying Barbara should come daily for two weeks and three times a week after that. Barbara said she racked up thirteen chiropractic visits with two or three chiropractors and five psychiatric appointments.

Lesley Stahl: "What did you say? Did you ever tell them that you did have back pain, neck pain? Did you ever feed their notions?"

Barbara: "I was asked every time I went in how I was feeling. And every time I went in, I said, 'I'm fine.' I had a headache one time. I did tell them I had a headache. But past that, I never complained of any back pain."

Stahl: "Never?"

Barbara: "Never."

Despite this, Barbara's insurance company received a report saying she was temporarily totally disabled. The insurance company also received two bills totaling $2,195. A legitimate chiropractor named Glenn Johnson examined Barbara and found nothing wrong with her whatsoever. She was, he said, "without any type of problem." Lesley Stahl asked Johnson about the other diagnosis. She wanted to know if this was fraud. "Yes," Johnson replied. "Flat out."

With this in mind, *60 Minutes* paid a visit to the chiropractic clinic that treated Barbara. The doctor in charge never showed up, but his wife denied any wrongdoing. Next, Lesley Stahl took the camera crew to the psychiatrist Barbara had seen. Stahl was able to get an interview with the doctor who had diagnosed Barbara as severely depressed. He recommended Barbara take lithium; she refused, and the doctor prescribed two other drugs, one of which was Sinequan. The doctor told Lesley Stahl that he saw Barbara was depressed, so he gave her a prescription.

Barbara, who was standing by listening to this exchange about her supposed state of mind, countered that she never said she was depressed, nor did she say she wanted drugs. "We had quite an argument about it, as a matter of fact," Barbara said. When the doctor was not there, Barbara repeated that she had not said she was depressed, nor was she anxious. "We laughed through the entire thing," she said. Barbara also told Lesley Stahl she did not say she had panic attacks. Stahl was asking about these specific items because the doctor's report to the insurance company concluded that Barbara had what were described as "major depression, panic disorder."

Lesley Stahl returned to the legal office where Barbara had been told how to make her claim in the first place. Stahl was accompanied by camera crews visible to all the world. It turned out that Rosie did not work at the office anymore and the man in charge wasn't in.

Lesley Stahl told the office manager that Barbara had been sent over to the office with nothing wrong with her, had been coached, and had come out with all sorts of symptoms she didn't have. With the correspondent standing in the doorway to her office, the manager calmly said that they merely went by what the client told them and no one would ever put words in a client's mouth. When Lesley Stahl said she had the coaching on tape, the manager suggested they return at four o'clock, when the owner was available.

The appointed time came and went, and *60 Minutes* called. The owner wasn't in then, and not at five or six either, and not three times the next day when *60 Minutes* called again. No one wanted to talk.

Among the medical professionals Lesley Stahl spoke with, there was frustration and anger that no action seemed to be taken to counteract this kind of abuse. Stahl asked Eugene Taylor if anyone had ever gone to jail for workers' compensation fraud.

Eugene Taylor: "I—I can't think of anybody that I know that has gone to jail for workers' compensation fraud."
Lesley Stahl: "Ever?"
Taylor: "Ever."
Stahl: "And all these years, and with all this money, and with all this scamming, nobody?"
Taylor: "Nobody."

In 2001, the California Commission on Health and Safety and Workers' Compensation reported that a drive against workers' comp fraud begun in the state in 1992 seemed to have led to a reduction in reported cases. The primary targets of the anti-fraud program were described as "medical treatment fraud, medical reporting fraud, claimant fraud, 'capping' by attorneys and others, and, ostensibly, employer and insurer fraud that discouraged or prevented injured workers from obtaining benefits. The program was subsequently broadened to include employer premium fraud."

A Few Minutes with Andy Rooney

:: May 19, 1999 ::

As tradition dictates, we finish up with a few choice words from Andy Rooney. Rooney is, as Mike Wallace said at the end of "The Best of Cons" special, the *60 Minutes* expert at blowing the whistle on the annoying things that get under all of our skin.

Andy Rooney: "Over the years, I've been irritated by a lot of business practices that are short of being really illegal."

For instance, he said, "you have to read any advertisement carefully." Take "double-occupancy," for example. A double-occupancy hotel room is advertised for $49. "Well, I called this number, and you pay $114 for this hotel room for one night. Not $49, because you can't get it for just one person."

::

And another thing: "Buying gas. That nine tenths of a cent is always annoying."

Unidentified gas station attendant: "That 96.9 is actually ninety-seven cents."
Rooney: "Well, it's not, actually."
Attendant: "Actually, it is: ninety-six and nine tenths is ninety-seven cents."
Rooney: "Well, why don't they say ninety-seven, then?"
Attendant: "Because the oil companies want to do it this way."

Take a closer look at your coffee can sometime, says Rooney. A can that used to contain sixteen ounces of coffee now has thirteen ounces. And the size of the print telling you how much coffee you're getting has also shrunk. Coincidence? Rooney thinks not.

::

"Does this look like a farm to you?" Rooney asks, standing in the midst of an unmistakably urban cityscape. "There's a place called Glenmere Farms not far from where we are right here in New York City." Pretty bucolic name for a company situated in the concrete jungle of Manhattan.

Rooney: "Are you with Glenmere Farms?"
Unidentified man: "Mm-hmmm."
Rooney: "Where are the cows?"
Man: "We don't have any cows."

Next, Rooney warns against judging a breakfast cereal by the cover of the box it comes in. Holding up the box of a breakfast cereal with blueberries, he notes that the blueberries on the box are gigantic, dwarfing any berry that might conceivably be found in nature.

One other cereal also has caught his attention: "This cereal called Fruity Pebbles, wouldn't you think it has fruit in it? Well it doesn't have fruit in it. Pebbles? I don't know."

::

Rooney then turns his critical eye to magazine gimmicks, declaring that even "good magazines use bad sales tricks." Some promotions seem to assume that readers are phenomenally gullible. "Look at this: Andrew Rooney wins $2 million," he says, showing an envelope from *Time* magazine with the proclamation printed on the front in bold letters. "Is there anyone smart enough to read *Time* magazine who's dumb enough to think he's won $2 million when he gets this?"

::

Finally, Rooney looks at Milli Vanilli, the singing duo that won a Grammy but was later proved to be lip-syncing to a sound track recorded by someone else. Their stunt inspires Rooney to try his hand at a Frank Sinatra impression. Microphone in hand, he voices the words to "You Make Me Feel So Young." If you can't beat 'em . . .

"It's hard to know why there are so many semihonest people in business," Rooney quips in conclusion, "and why the rest of us are such suckers."

60 Minutes is the only television broadcast to be the most-watched show in America in three separate decades. Since its debut in 1968, the critically celebrated program has won seventy-three Emmy Awards—the most for any news program—as well as nine Peabody Awards for exceptional television broadcasting. According to Nielsen, nearly fifteen million viewers tuned in to the show every Sunday evening during the 2001–2002 season.